中国思想文化术语多语种对外翻译
标准化建设项目成果
CHINESE THINKING AND CULTURE
MULTILINGUAL TERMINOLOGY DATABASE

中华源·河南故事
CHINESE CIVILIZATION
Stories from Henan

黄帝
HUANGDI (THE YELLOW EMPEROR)

河南省人民政府外事办公室　编

河南大学出版社
HENAN UNIVERSITY PRESS
·郑州·

图书在版编目（CIP）数据

中华源·河南故事. 黄帝：汉、英 / 河南省人民政府外事办公室编. -- 郑州：河南大学出版社，2021.4（2023.10重印）

ISBN 978-7-5649-4668-5

Ⅰ. ①中… Ⅱ. ①河… Ⅲ. ①地方文化－河南－通俗读物－汉、英②黄帝－传记－通俗读物－汉、英 Ⅳ. ①G127.61-49②K827=1

中国版本图书馆CIP数据核字（2021）第076655号

责任编辑	林方丽
责任校对	阮林耍
封面设计	翟淼淼
出版发行	河南大学出版社
	地址：郑州市郑东新区商务外环中华大厦2401号　邮编：450046
	电话：0371-86059701（营销部）
	0371-86059750（高等教育与职业教育分公司）
	网址：hupress.henu.edu.cn
排　版	河南大学出版社设计排版部
印　刷	河南博雅彩印有限公司
版　次	2021年4月第1版　　印　次　2023年10月第2次印刷
开　本	710 mm×1010 mm　1/16　印　张　11.5
字　数	184千字　　　　　　　定　价　56.00元

版权所有，侵权必究

本书如有印装质量问题，请与河南大学出版社营销部联系调换。

"中华源·河南故事"系列丛书编委会

顾　　问	黄友义　杨　平　范大祺
名誉主任	穆为民　何金平　刘炯天
主　　任	付　静
副 主 任	陈　岩　陈志伟　刁玉华　方启雄　介晓磊 孔留安　李冰冰　李向前　李　镇　梁留科 刘金锋　牛卫国　屈鹏飞　史永庆　田　凯 万正峰　王建修　王清义　王自文　许二平 杨建伟　杨玮斌　张改平　张俊峰　张明超 张松文　赵卫东
主　　编	付　静
副 主 编	李冰冰
编　　委	陈　玮　丁　锐　高　阳　徐恒振　郑延保

中华源·河南故事·黄帝

主　　编	牛卫国
副 主 编	马志峰　潘新红　郭万群（英文）
中文撰稿	张天伟　刘宏民　牛青山　柴高洁　任永安
英文译者	涂晓韦　王惠瑜　闫秋霞　龚梦南
英文审校	〔加拿大〕Corey Ross Cole
摄　　影	刘宏民　刘栓阳　刘明甫　李伟彬　靳炎生　梁伟平
绘　　画	孙小朵

The Editorial Committee
Chinese Civilization
Stories from Henan

Consultants	Huang Youyi Yang Ping Fan Daqi
Honorary Directors	Mu Weimin He Jinping Liu Jiongtian
Director	Fu Jing
Deputy Directors	Chen Yan Chen Zhiwei Diao Yuhua Fang Qixiong
	Jie Xiaolei Kong Liu'an Li Bingbing Li Xiangqian
	Li Zhen Liang Liuke Liu Jinfeng Niu Weiguo
	Qu Pengfei Shi Yongqing Tian Kai Wan Zhengfeng
	Wang Jianxiu Wang Qingyi Wang Ziwen Xu Erping
	Yang Jianwei Yang Weibin Zhang Gaiping
	Zhang Junfeng Zhang Mingchao Zhang Songwen
	Zhao Weidong
Chief Editor	Fu Jing
Deputy Chief Editor	Li Bingbing
Editors	Chen Wei Ding Rui Gao Yang Xu Hengzhen
	Zheng Yanbao

Chinese Civilization
Stories from Henan
Huangdi (*The Yellow Emperor*)

Editor-in-Chief	Niu Weiguo
Associate Editors-in-Chief	Ma Zhifeng Pan Xinhong Guo Wanqun (English Text)
Writers	Zhang Tianwei Liu Hongmin Niu Qingshan
	Chai Gaojie Ren Yongan
Translators	Tu Xiaowei Wang Huiyu Yan Qiuxia Gong Mengnan
Translation Proofreader	Corey Ross Cole (Canada)
Photographers	Liu Hongmin Liu Shuanyang Liu Mingfu
	Li Weibin Jin Yansheng Liang Weiping
Painter	Sun Xiaoduo

总　序

中国是世界四大文明古国之一，也是世界上唯一的古代文明传统未曾中断的国家。河南省地处中国中东部，是中华文明和中华民族的重要发祥地，在中国五千年的文明史上，河南作为国家政治、经济、文化的中心就长达三千多年。从某种意义上讲，一部河南史就是半部中国史。这里是中华人文始祖黄帝的故乡，是古丝绸之路的东方起点，是少林功夫和陈氏太极的发源地，这里创建了中国历史上最早的都城，镌刻了中国最古老的文字，诞生了中国最初的商业文明。

伴随着新时代的荣光，河南经济社会发展迅速，人民生活水平显著提升，这是河南人民自力更生、艰苦奋斗的历史结果，也是对外开放带来的益处。河南经济社会的发展、人民生活方式的改变都植根于深层次的文化积淀。为了让世界更多地了解河南，让河南更好地走向世界，2018年以来，河南省人民政府外事办公室认真研析了这片古老土地上的历史文化资源和时代风貌，组织各领域权威专家学者，编译了"中华源·河南故事"中外文系列丛书，选取黄河文化、河洛文化、老子、庄子、黄帝、少林功夫、太极拳、中医、汉字、丝绸之路、古都、农业、大运河、文物、陶瓷、青铜器、手工艺、书法、杂技、豫菜、豫剧、脱贫攻坚、空中丝绸之路、航空城、南水北调、中原粮谷、红旗渠、焦裕禄等多个主题，力图以故事的方式向世界展现一个立体、全面、真实的河南。

当今世界，人类文明无论是在物质还是在精神方面都取得了巨大进步，特别是物质的极大丰富，这在古代世界是完全不能想象的。同时，当代人类也面临着许多突出的难题，比如，贫富差距持续扩大，物欲追求奢华无度，个人主义恶性膨胀，社会诚信不断消减，伦理道德每况愈下，人与自然关系日趋紧张，等等。要解决这些难题，不仅需要运用人类今天的智慧和力量，而且需要运用人类历史上积累和储存的智慧和力量。河南历史文化底蕴深厚、包容性强，在今天仍极具现实意义。中原文化蕴含的思想智慧有助于修身养性，推动人类社会进步发展，焦裕禄精神、红旗渠精神所体现的为民爱民、艰苦奋斗的价值取向是构建人类命运共同体的力量源泉。我们期待与读者们一起从河南故事中汲取更多的智慧和力量，共同创造更加美好的未来。

Series Foreword

China is one of the four ancient civilizations in the world, and is also the only country in the world where the ancient civilization has not been interrupted. Located in east-central China, Henan Province is an important cradle for the Chinese nation and Chinese civilization. In the course of the five thousand years of Chinese history, for more than three thousand years it served as the political, economic and cultural center of the country and therefore, as generally accepted, represents half of the history of China. Henan is the native place of Yellow Emperor, the cradle of Chinese culture, the starting point of the ancient Silk Road in the east, and the birthplace of Shaolin Kungfu and Chen-style Taijiquan—typical examples of the world-renowned Chinese martial arts. It was here that the earliest capital city in China was founded, the oldest Chinese characters engraved, and the earliest commerce took shape.

In the new era, Henan has witnessed rapid growth in its economy and remarkable improvement of people's living conditions owing to the national reform and opening-up policy and unremitting endeavors of the people. Modern economic achievements and social development as well as the changes of way of life could be traced back to its traditional values and cultural heritages. To enable people from other countries to understand Henan, and let the Province integrate more efficiently into the world development, the Foreign Affairs Office of the People's Government of Henan Province has organized teams of authoritative experts and scholars in relevant fields to compile this *Chinese Civilization: Stories from Henan* in Chinese and foreign languages since 2018 by crystallizing the excellence of traditions and outstanding features of modern development. The book series include *The Yellow River Culture*, *Heluo Culture*, *Laozi*, *Zhuangzi*, *The Yellow Emperor*, *Shaolin Kungfu*, *Taijiquan*, *Traditional Chinese Medicine*,

Chinese Characters, *The Silk Road*, *Ancient Chinese Capitals*, *Feeding the People—Agriculture*, *The Grand Canal*, *Cultural Heritage*, *Ceramic*, *Bronze*, *Handicraft Art*, *Calligraphy*, *Acrobatics*, *Henan Cuisine*, *Henan Opera*, *Poverty Alleviation*, *Silk Road in the Air*, *Zhengzhou—An Aviation City*, *South-to-North Water Diversion*, *Grain of the Central Plains*, *Man-Made River—Hongqiqu Canal*, *A Model Official—Jiao Yulu*, etc., presenting a panoramic picture of the Province.

In today's world, human civilization has made great progress in both material accumulation and ethical advancement, and the great abundance of materials today, especially, is beyond the imagination of the ancient people. At the same time, however, modern people are also confronted with a lot of problems, such as the widening gap between the rich and the poor, the indulgence in pursuit of luxury and extravagance, the undesirable extension of individualism, the decline of social integrity, and the increasingly tense relationship between man and nature. To solve the problems, we need to draw on the wisdom and powers developed today as well as those accumulated in the past. Henan is endowed with rich historical and cultural heritages characterized by its inclusiveness, and such heritages remain significant today. The intelligence and wisdom in Henan culture are conducive to self-cultivation and to the promotion of social development. The spirit of serving the people and relentless struggle, as embodied in Jiao Yulu and the man-made river—Hongqiqu Canal provides source of strength for building a community with a shared future for mankind. It is our hope that wisdom and strength from Henan stories could lead us to a shared brilliant future.

前　言

　　轩辕黄帝是中华民族人文始祖，生于五千多年前的中国中原地区有熊国轩辕丘。司马迁《史记·五帝本纪》开宗把黄帝列为"五帝"之首，他是有熊国的开国之君。

　　《庄子》说："世之所高，莫若黄帝。"轩辕黄帝既是远古中华从野蛮走向文明所取得一切成就的集大成者，又是中华文明的开创者；既是"邦国古国"的统一者，又是大同社会的建立者；既是中华民族的缔造者，又是中华文化的创立者。黄帝文化是中国的根源文化，是中华文明的精髓和活的灵魂，它不但为后人奠定了正确认识世界的世界观和方法论，而且为人们奠定了勇于改造世界的价值观和实践论。

　　黄帝文化是从中国土壤里生长起来的文化，并形成了自己的特色和优势，既具原创性又具传承性，更彰显时代性，是支撑中华民族生存、发展的精神支柱，是推动中华民族走向复兴、繁荣的强大精神动力。

　　五千多年前，黄帝修德振兵、习用干戈、以征不享，通过阪泉之战、涿鹿之战，结束了远古中国长期纷争的局面，使得早期邦国、古国社会进入以王朝为标志的国家历史新纪元。轩辕黄帝是中国国家缔造者。在统一的国家制度下，他有力地促进了社会生产、科学技术、文化艺术等各方面的大发展，使中华民族进入文明时代。

　　黄帝文化的传承弘扬从未中断，历朝历代祭拜黄帝也从未停止。孙中山、毛泽东都有诗文、祭文高度评价轩辕黄帝的伟大功绩。2008年，"新郑黄帝拜祖祭典"经国务院批准列入国家级非物质文化遗产名录。2012年,黄帝故里拜祖大典荣膺"全球最具影响力十大根亲文化盛事"。每年农历三月三,中国大陆和中国港、澳、台及世界各地华人都以不同形式拜谒轩辕黄帝,体现了文化寻根的民族情结和中华民族的礼仪内涵,极大增强了中华民族的凝聚力、向心力和亲和力,对构建和谐社会,培育民族精神,增强民族团结,维护祖国统一,实现中华民族伟大复兴的中国梦起着重要的促进作用。

本书不仅是对远古中华文化的历史追忆,更是对黄帝文化的传承和弘扬。黄帝的思想和功绩记录在传世典籍中,更流淌在后人的文宗血脉里,为中华民族的文化自信提供了强大支撑。

本书分为黄帝其人其事、黄帝治国方略、黄帝文化传承和黄帝精神弘扬四个篇章,讲述了黄帝统一万邦、建立国家、创造中华文明的光辉历程和事迹。它对于人们了解远古中华历史,弘扬中华传统文化,促进新时代文化建设,构建人类命运共同体,具有重要的指导和借鉴意义。

Preface

Xuanyuan Huangdi, known as the Yellow Emperor and the ancestor of Chinese humanities, was born more than 5,000 years ago at Xuanyuan Hill of the Youxiong Kingdom in the Central Plains of China. He was the founder of Youxiong, and was listed as the first of the "Five Emperors" in *The Records of the Grand Historian* by Sima Qian.

Zhuangzi states, "There is none higher in the world than Huangdi." Huangdi is not only the master of all the achievements of ancient China from its barbaric to civilized periods, but also the founder of Chinese civilization, as well as the Chinese nation and culture; in his time, he was the unifier of all the vassals and the founder of a harmonious society. Regarded as the root culture of China, Huangdi culture is the essence and living soul of Chinese civilization. It establishes not only the perspective and methodology for descendants to understand the world, but also the values and practical theory for people to transform the world.

Grown in Chinese soil, Huangdi culture has formed its own characteristics and advantages and has enriched itself with originality, heritage, and contemporaneity. It serves as a spiritual pillar to support the survival and development of the Chinese nation, and a strong ideological motivation to promote the Chinese nation toward rejuvenation and prosperity.

More than 5,000 years ago, Huangdi cultivated virtue and revitalized the army, using the art of battle formation to conquer vassals who did not make offerings. Through the battles of Banquan and Zhuolu, he ended the long-standing strife in ancient China, allowing the ancient society to enter a new era of national history marked by dynasties. Thus, Huangdi became the first founder of the Chinese nation. The unified state system promoted the great progress in social production, science and technology, culture and art in all aspects and brought the Chinese nation into an age of civilization.

The inheritance and promotion of Huangdi culture remain uninterrupted, and the worship of Huangdi has never ceased throughout successive dynasties. Sun Yat-sen and Mao Zedong both wrote poems and elegiac addresses that spoke highly of Huangdi's achievements. The Xinzheng Yellow Emperor Worship Ceremony was approved by the State Council for inclusion in the National List of Intangible Cultural Heritage in 2008 and honored among the top 10 most influential root culture events in the world in 2012. Every year, on March 3 of the lunar calendar, the Chinese people around the world pay homage to Huangdi in various forms, reflecting the national sentiment around the cultural roots and the ritual connotations of the Chinese nation. This ceremony greatly enhances the cohesion, centripetal force, and affinity of China and thus plays an important role in building a harmonious society, cultivating national spirit, bolstering national unity, maintaining the unity of the motherland and realizing the Chinese dream of the great rejuvenation of the nation.

This book is not only a historical reminiscence about ancient Chinese culture, but also an illustration of the inheritance and promotion of Huangdi culture. Huangdi's thoughts and achievements have been recorded in heirloom texts and run in the literary and patriotic bloodline of his descendants, providing strong support for the cultural confidence of the Chinese nation.

This book consists of four chapters, namely, Chapter 1 The Story of Huangdi, Chapter 2 Huangdi's Strategies of Governance, Chapter 3 Inheritance of Huangdi Culture, and Chapter 4 Promotion of Huangdi Spirit (i.e. his ideologies central to his legacy). It presents the glorious history and stories about how he unified the tribes, established the kingdom, and created Chinese civilization. It is an important guidance and reference for people to understand ancient Chinese history, enhance traditional Chinese culture, promote the cultural construction of a new era, and develop a community with a shared future for mankind.

目　录　　　　　　　　　　　　　Contents

第一章　黄帝其人其事 ……………………………………… 001
　一、生于轩辕之丘 …………………………………………… 002
　二、继任有熊国君 …………………………………………… 004
　三、建立炎黄联盟 …………………………………………… 008
　四、决胜涿鹿之战 …………………………………………… 010
　五、实现万邦一统 …………………………………………… 014
　六、建国立都有熊 …………………………………………… 018
　七、创造华夏文明 …………………………………………… 022

Chapter 1　The Story of Huangdi ……………………………… 001
　Ⅰ. Birth at Xuanyuan Hill ……………………………………… 003
　Ⅱ. Succession to the Throne …………………………………… 005
　Ⅲ. Foundation of the Yan Huang Alliance …………………… 009
　Ⅳ. Victory of the Zhuolu Battle ……………………………… 011
　Ⅴ. Realization of Unification ………………………………… 015
　Ⅵ. Establishment of the Capital in Youxiong ………………… 019
　Ⅶ. Creation of Chinese Civilization …………………………… 023

第二章　黄帝治国方略 ……………………………………… 031
　一、以人为本的执政理念 …………………………………… 032
　二、德法兼治的治国方略 …………………………………… 048
　三、和而不同的处世方法 …………………………………… 056
　四、以文化人的教化思想 …………………………………… 062
　五、黄帝的人文科学思想 …………………………………… 068

| Chapter 2 | Huangdi's Strategies of Governance | 031 |

　　Ⅰ. People-Oriented Governing Philosophy　　　　　　　033
　　Ⅱ. Governing by Morality and Law　　　　　　　　　　049
　　Ⅲ. Harmonious but Different Approaches to the World　　057
　　Ⅳ. Ideal of Educating People with Culture　　　　　　　063
　　Ⅴ. Huangdi's Thought of Humanistic Science　　　　　　069

第三章　黄帝文化传承　　　　　　　　　　　　　　　　081

　　一、黄帝文化在中国历史上的影响　　　　　　　　　　082
　　二、历代祭拜黄帝　　　　　　　　　　　　　　　　　092
　　三、黄帝文化研究　　　　　　　　　　　　　　　　　100
　　四、黄帝文化传播　　　　　　　　　　　　　　　　　108

Chapter 3　Inheritance of Huangdi Culture　　　　　　　081

　　Ⅰ. Influence of Huangdi Culture in Chinese History　　　083
　　Ⅱ. Worship of Huangdi in All Dynasties　　　　　　　　093
　　Ⅲ. Research on Huangdi Culture　　　　　　　　　　　101
　　Ⅳ. Spread of Huangdi Culture　　　　　　　　　　　　109

第四章　黄帝精神弘扬　　　　　　　　　　　　　　　　119

　　一、自强不息的奋斗精神　　　　　　　　　　　　　　120
　　二、革故鼎新的创造精神　　　　　　　　　　　　　　126
　　三、厚德载物的仁德精神　　　　　　　　　　　　　　130
　　四、天下为公的正大精神　　　　　　　　　　　　　　138
　　五、以人为本的人文精神　　　　　　　　　　　　　　144
　　六、中和大同的和谐精神　　　　　　　　　　　　　　154

Chapter 4　Promotion of Huangdi Spirit　　　　　　　　　　　　　119
　　　　　Ⅰ. Spirit of Endless Self-Improvement　　　　　　　121
　　　　　Ⅱ. Spirit of Innovation　　　　　　　　　　　　　127
　　　　　Ⅲ. Spirit of Clemency　　　　　　　　　　　　　131
　　　　　Ⅳ. Spirit of Equality　　　　　　　　　　　　　139
　　　　　Ⅴ. People-Oriented Spirit　　　　　　　　　　　145
　　　　　Ⅵ. Spirit of Great Unity　　　　　　　　　　　155

附录：中国历史年代简表　　　　　　　　　　　　　　　　　164
Appendix : A Brief Chronology of Chinese History　　　　　　164

第一章

黄帝其人其事

Chapter 1

The Story of Huangdi

一、生于轩辕之丘

五千多年前的一个春天,有熊国君少典的妻子附宝生下一个男婴。由于生于轩辕丘(今河南新郑),少典就给他取名轩辕。轩辕成长于姬水河畔,爹娘就给他定姓为姬。姬轩辕自幼聪明伶俐,学什么会什么,而且能举一反三,触类旁通。

少典对轩辕寄予很大希望,就让有熊国最有学问的人做他的师父,这个人叫作大项。大项给轩辕讲天文、地理、有熊国的历史和做人的道理。几年间,轩辕学到不少知识,大项师父十分满意。

后来,少典把轩辕送往外地学艺。轩辕先后学于封钜、岐伯、力牧子等人,学识更为渊博。

轩辕诞生
Birth of Xuanyuan

Ⅰ. Birth at Xuanyuan Hill

One spring, about 5,000 years ago, Fubao, the wife of Shaodian (ruler of Youxiong), gave birth to a baby boy at Xuanyuan Hill (presently located in Xinzheng, Henan Province) and therefore Shaodian named the boy Xuanyuan. Because he grew up by the Jishui River, he was entitled the surname Ji. Ji Xuanyuan was a gifted child who understood everything quickly and was good at inference and analogy based on what he had learned.

Shaodian had high expectations for Xuanyuan and made Daxiang, the most learned man in the Youxiong Kingdom, his master. Daxiang lectured Xuanyuan on astronomy, geography, the history of the Youxiong Kingdom and the philosophy of being a man. Within a few years, Xuanyuan mastered many things to Daxiang's great satisfaction.

Later, Shaodian sent Xuanyuan from his hometown to learn from scholars such as Fengju, Qibo, and Limuzi, and increased his knowledge.

轩辕黄帝塑像
Statue of Xuanyuan Huangdi

二、继任有熊国君

学成归来的轩辕,已经是一个文武双全、心怀天下、具有远大理想的英武青年。他看到天下大乱,野蛮横行,征伐无度,人民的生命受到极大的摧残,立志要改变这一野蛮的世界。

为实现自己的抱负,他组建起一个全新的轩辕部落。无论天南海北,凡是有德、有才、有智的贤智之人均可参加。不足一年,加入轩辕部落的已超过百人。

父亲少典见轩辕志向远大、德才兼备、能力超群,心中高兴,便将国君的职位传于他。姬轩辕继任了父亲少典的职位,当上了有熊国君。轩辕当上有熊国君后,娶西陵氏的女子嫘祖为妻。嫘祖带领民众种桑养蚕,缫丝织帛,让民众都穿上了丝制的衣裳。轩辕和嫘祖生下两个儿子,一个叫玄嚣,一个叫昌意。二人长大后,都有了封地。

嫘祖
Leizu

为了防止外来势力的侵扰,轩辕又联络其他部族,组成有熊联盟,并被推选为联盟盟主。大项、大隗、天老为联盟谋师,沮诵、隶首等五十余人各司其职。联盟又成立了一支拥有三千余人的军队,长期进行

II. Succession to the Throne

After completing his study, Xuanyuan became an ambitious young man who was not only talented in arts and swords but also embodied a high vision of governing the kingdom. Witnessing the chaos of his country and the suffering of his people, he was determined to change the barbaric world.

To realize his ambition, he established a new tribe called Xuanyuan which welcomed all virtuous, talented, and wise people to join in, regardless of their identity or hometown. As a result, more than a hundred people joined the tribe within a year.

Delighted to see Xuanyuan's outstanding ability and profound knowledge, Shaodian joyfully handed over the throne to him. Ji Xuanyuan succeeded his father as the emperor of Youxiong. After the enthronement, Xuanyuan married Leizu from the Xiling clan. Leizu taught the people how to raise silkworms and make silk so that they had silk clothes to wear at that time. Xuanyuan and Leizu had two sons, one named Xuanxiao and the other Changyi. When they grew up, both sons were given fiefdoms.

黄帝屯兵洞内景
Interior of Huangdi's Army Garrison Cave

黄帝屯兵洞
Huangdi's Army Garrison Cave

军事训练，防患于未然。轩辕知道，当下世界，危机四伏，强欺弱，众暴寡，部落纷争，强盗肆行，天下百姓身处灾难之中。所以，他审时度势，实施仁道，为民立命，以德依法治理联盟。为了有熊联盟的强大和发展，他联合一切可以联合的力量，齐心协力，同甘共苦，为创造一个天下一统、人民幸福的祥和社会而努力。他思贤若渴，不远千里到东方寻找风后、力牧，并将他们迎接到有熊联盟，举行盛大的拜将仪式。仪式上，轩辕恭敬站立，向风后、力牧深鞠三躬，拜风后为相，拜力牧为将军。

To prevent the invasion of external forces, Xuanyuan allied with other tribes, set up the Youxiong Alliance and was elected as its leader. Daxiang, Dawei and Tianlao served as the alliance strategists, while Jusong, Lishou and approximately 50 other members performed additional roles. The alliance established an army of more than 3,000 soldiers and organized long-term military training to guard against unforeseen troubles. Xuanyuan was well aware of the trials of the world around him; dangers lurked, the stronger and larger ones bullied the rest, clashes and crimes occurred among tribes, and people's lives were miserable. Judging from this situation, he implemented benevolence, improved the people's quality of life, and ruled the alliance by law, with virtue and kindness. To strengthen and develop the Youxiong Alliance, he unified all the forces that could be united to work hard together to create a harmonious society in which people could live happily. He greatly desired for the support of the wise and travelled all the way to the east to find Fenghou and Limu and ask them to join the alliance. At a grand ceremony held to bestow Fenghou the position of prime minister and Limu that of general, Xuanyuan bowed three times to them to show his respect.

三、建立炎黄联盟

随着姬轩辕在各氏族部落中的威望逐渐提升和有熊联盟的不断壮大，炎帝联盟中许多部落、方国纷纷投奔有熊联盟。炎帝榆罔非常气愤，于是，他率领军队，与有熊联盟军展开大战。

轩辕率军队以雕鹖鹰鸢为旗帜，以熊罴貔虎（指作战勇士）为前驱，与炎帝联盟军战于阪泉之野。经过三次激烈战斗，有熊联盟军取得最终胜利。阪泉之战结束后，在轩辕的倡导下，建立了炎黄联盟。从此，中原地区部落、方国间长期纷争的局面得以平息。

炎黄结盟
Yan Huang Alliance

III. Foundation of the Yan Huang Alliance

As Ji Xuanyuan's prestige among the clans and tribes gradually increased and the Youxiong Alliance continued to grow, many tribes and states in the Yandi Alliance defected to the Youxiong Alliance. This shift deeply angered Yandi (Yan Emperor) Yuwang, prompting him to lead his army in a great battle against the Youxiong Alliance.

With Diao, He, Ying and Zhan (four kinds of birds) as their flag and Xiong, Pi, Chu and Hu (four animal totems as warriors) as their forerunner, the Xuanyuan tribe fought in the wilderness of Banquan against the Yandi Alliance. After three fierce battles, the Youxiong Alliance prevailed. As the Battle of Banquan ended, the Yan Huang Alliance was formed under Xuanyuan's advocacy. Eventually, the long-running conflicts among tribes and states in the Central Plains ceased.

轩辕黄帝塑像
Statue of Xuanyuan Huangdi

四、决胜涿鹿之战

涿鹿之战是轩辕率领的有熊联盟军联合炎帝联盟军与蚩尤率领的九黎联军,在涿鹿(今河北省涿鹿地区)进行的一场大战。据典籍记载,涿鹿之战时间长达三年,先后经过五十二次战斗才结束。本次战争以有熊、炎帝联军胜利,九黎联军失败而告终。

涿鹿之战
Zhuolu Battle

在涿鹿之战中,轩辕率军队抢占有利地形,将蚩尤军队牢牢围困在山谷之中。为适应雾天作战,轩辕令风后研制指南车,以辨别方向。又令风后演"河图"、创"遁甲"(古代道家预测学,方士术数之一),以推主客胜负之术。轩辕作"胜负握机之图"及"出军新用诀",以备攻战。他把握总攻击的时间、地点,迫使蚩尤军北逃进入谷口,在山谷生擒了蚩尤,并解散了九黎联盟军队。

Ⅳ. Victory of the Zhuolu Battle

The Zhuolu Battle took place in Zhuolu (presently located in Zhuolu, Hebei Province) between the Xuanyuan-led coalition forces of the Youxiong Alliance Army and Yandi Alliance Army and the Chiyou-led Jiuli Allied Forces. According to ancient records, the battle lasted for three years and involved fifty-two military actions; the victory finally went to the coalition forces of the Youxiong Alliance and Yandi Alliance.

In the Zhuolu Battle, Xuanyuan directed his soldiers to take the vantage points, and trapped Chiyou's army in the valley. He ordered Fenghou to develop a compass chariot capable of detecting direction on foggy days in combat. He also asked Fenghou to draw a river map *Hetu* and practised *Dunjia* (a predictive methodology and divination in Taoism) to obtain strategies to win the battle. To prepare for the attack, he wrote *Chart of Victory over Defeat* and *New Military Strategies* as guidance for his army. By ascertaining the right time and location for the attack, Xuanyuan forced Chiyou's army to retreat north into the mouth of the valley, where Chiyou was captured alive and the Jiuli Allied Forces was disbanded.

黄帝祠
Ancestral Hall of Huangdi

涿鹿之战是中国远古史上所发生的最大战役。此次战争的爆发是由九黎联盟军攻打炎帝联盟军，将炎帝联盟军驱赶到涿鹿盆地实施围攻所引起的。起初由于炎帝联盟军和九黎军队在军事力量上的悬殊，炎帝联盟军陷入十分被动的境地。在此情况下，轩辕率领有熊军队赶赴涿鹿，与炎帝联盟军汇合，勠力同心，与九黎联军展开了历史性决战。轩辕挥师北上，援救炎帝联盟军共击九黎联军，为的是以战止战，最终消除战争，建立起社会新秩序。涿鹿之战促进了部族之间的融合，为早期中国的建立奠定了坚实基础。

中天阁
Zhongtian Pavilion

The Zhuolu Battle, the largest battle in the history of ancient China, originated from the Jiuli Allied Forces' attack on the Yandi Alliance, which was later besieged in the Zhuolu Basin. Due to the great disparity in power between the two sides, the Yandi Alliance was forced into a dire situation. Under these circumstances, a historical battle was recorded when the Youxiong army joined the Yandi Alliance to fight hard together against the Jiuli Allied Forces. The coalition fight that Xuanyuan conducted aimed to end the war permanently and build a new social order. Having already promoted the integration of diverse tribes, the Zhuolu Battle laid a solid foundation for the establishment of early China.

五、实现万邦一统

涿鹿之战结束后,北方的荤粥族又出兵南侵,轩辕率军队反击,又令军将率兵征伐天下四方作乱者,最终平息了天下纷争。轩辕在釜山大会诸侯,举行"合符"仪式,接受军将、大臣、诸侯交回的玉符,从此结束了世间长期纷争的局面,天下归为一统。轩辕以平叛之功,令岐伯作军乐之歌,谓箫铙歌,然后率军队回归有熊。

己酉年春月,西太山(今河南省新郑市龙湖镇)上龙旗飘扬,鼓乐阵阵,万民欢畅,会盟大会隆重举行。轩辕得到四方诸侯的拥戴,被推举为天子。

西太山黄帝会盟祠
Temple for the Yellow Emperor's Alliance in Xitaishan Mountain

轩辕黄帝在即位仪式上发表演说,他说:"我的德行禀赋于上天,即位受意于大地,事业功成乃得于民心。因为我的德行可比配天地,所以可在人间设立天子、封建国家、分封诸侯,并分别为他们配置三公、

V. Realization of Unification

After the Zhuolu Battle, Xuanyuan's army defeated Xunyu, a northern tribe that had invaded the south. Xuanyuan further ordered his generals to conquer the rebellious tribes in the region and finally put an end to all clashes. Xuanyuan held a grand ceremony of Hefu at Fushan Mountain to receive all the jade tallies that he had given to the generals, ministers, and vassals. From that point on, the long period of disputes were over, and the nation was completely united. To celebrate the success of the counterinsurgency, Xuanyuan asked Qibo to perform a military

轩辕宫（三宫）
Xuanyuan Palace (Three Palaces)

三卿等各级官吏。我通过对日、月、年数的推算制定历法，使之合乎日、月的运行规律。"

黄帝以土德之瑞而王天下。"黄"为土色而象征土，所以，便有了"黄帝"的称谓。黄帝仰可取象于天，俯可取度于地，中可取法于人。他的即位盟辞也彰显出"天人合一"的思想。

轩辕庙
Xuanyuan Temple

song called *The Song of Xiaonao*; he then led his army back to Youxiong.

In the spring of the year Jiyou (one of the branches of the lunar calendar, the 46th in order), the Alliance Meeting was held at Xitaishan Mountain (presently located in Longhu Town, Xinzheng City, Henan Province) with the dragon flags fluttering, drums and music playing, and all the people celebrating. Deeply supported by all the vassals, Xuanyuan was elected Tianzi (emperor, the son of heaven).

At his coronation ceremony, the Yellow Emperor made the following speech, "I received my virtues from heaven, throne from the earth and career success from the people. Because my morality can match heaven and earth, I established Tianzi, the feudal country and vassas, the three-levelled administration, and gave them each Sangong (top three officials for the management of a country) and Sanqing (Situ, Sima and Sikong, three important official titles in ancient China). I have established the calendar based on the calculation and observation of days, months, and years to fit the motion laws of the sun and the moon."

Huangdi ascended the throne due to his fate on earth. As the Chinese character "huang" (yellow) is the color of earth, he was named Huangdi (the Yellow Emperor). Capable of reading the motion of the sky, estimating the movement of the earth, and making laws by observing the people, he manifested the spirit of harmony between man and nature in his coronation speech.

六、建国立都有熊

黄帝建国立都于有熊。以云纪官。设立二监、三公、四史、五官、六相、七辅、九士、十一将、二十官。各种司职官员达到百余人。这些官员都是各地推举出的思想家、政治家、谋略家、军事家和各行各业的杰出代表。

黄帝建都有熊。疆域南至交趾,北至幽陵,西至流沙,东及蟠木。

黄帝上观天文,大行时令,周游天下,以察地理,于是划野分州,故"井一为邻,邻三为朋,朋三为里,里五为邑,邑十为都,都十为师,师十为州"。行政建制分为九级,即中央、州、师、都、邑、里、朋、邻、井。

黄帝建立起完备的管理体制,并有国号、国都和行政、军队、司法等各级管理机构,揭开了华夏民族发展的新篇章。

高举龙旗
Holding the Dragon Flag High

VI. Establishment of the Capital in Youxiong

Youxiong (presently located in Xinzheng, Henan Province) was made the capital of Huangdi's empire, and all the officials were named with the character Yun. Huangdi set up more than a hundred administrative officials, including Jian (监), Gong (公), Shi (史), Guan (官), Xiang (相), Fu (辅), Shi (士), Jiang (将), and Guan (官), who were elected from among thinkers, politicians, tacticians, strategists, and other outstanding representatives from various professions.

The territory of the Youxiong Kingdom reached Jiaozhi in the south, Youling in the north, Liusha in the west and Panmu in the east.

Owing to his astronomical considerations, Huangdi greatly promoted the concept of seasons. Based on his geological observation after travelling around the country, he divided the administration into the following nine levels (from bottom to top): Jing, Lin (equaling one Jing), Peng (consisting of three Lin), Li (three Peng), Yi (five Li), Du (ten Yi), Shi (ten Du), Zhou (ten Shi) and the central government.

建都有熊
Youxiong, the Capital

天中门石坊
Stone Archway of Tianzhong Gate

  黄帝分封了许多诸侯国,并为它们配置三公、官吏,帮助发展农牧业。四方的诸侯国与有熊国进行文化上的交流与融合,共同开创了史无前例的大一统局面。

By establishing a complete administrative system with the state title, capital, and different levels of administrative, military, and judicial management institutions, Huangdi opened a new chapter on the development of the Chinese nation.

Along with three Gong and other officials, Huangdi enfeoffed many vassal states to help develop agriculture and animal husbandry. The cultural exchange between those vassal states and the Youxiong Kingdom created an unprecedented unification.

天中门
Tianzhong Gate

七、创造华夏文明

黄帝倡导社会公平、正义、和谐。他从人的道德修养，到如何调节人的"喜、怒、哀、乐、惧、恐、惊"等方面对民众进行教化。并设九德之臣，以德示范于人民。行十义之教，即"君仁、臣忠，父慈、子孝，兄良、弟悌，夫义、妇听，长惠、幼顺"。又制礼乐，实施以德治国。

自黄帝妃嫘祖、嫫母发明了养蚕、缫丝、织帛技术后，民众都穿上了用蚕丝做的衣服。黄帝又建立衣服制度，以礼示范天下，称"垂裳"。根据朝内大臣官职的不同，以服装加以区别。他让胡曹、伯余为自己做了一件朝服，供上朝时穿用。朝服上绣日月星辰以象天，又绣龙纹，称为龙服。伶伦是有名的音乐大师，创作了《龙衮之颂》歌曲，歌颂黄帝垂衣裳而治天下的功绩。

伶伦是黄帝的乐官。他往大夏之西昆仑嶰谷，采龙钟之竹，做成竹笛，吹之为黄钟之音。黄帝推行音乐教化，不仅在于表达人们的悲喜哀乐，还在于彰显美德、感恩报情、表达和平和谐情感，使人们的心灵得到调养。

黄帝既得"龙凤之图"，又得"河图""洛书"（指远古时代人们按照星象排布出时间、方向和季节的辨别系统），即让仓颉、沮诵创造文字。仓颉是黄帝的史官。他自从到了有熊国，就收集各个部落的陶器符号、文符、图画等，大大丰富了造字的内容，经过多年研究，终于造出了文字。

仓颉造出了文字，可做文章、书契，取代了结绳记事。轩辕就用文字定名百物，决断万事。一些迷信鬼神的女巫，都吓得躲藏起来，再也不敢随意欺骗百姓了。

VII. Creation of Chinese Civilization

Huangdi advocated social equality, justice, and harmony, educated people in moral cultivation and moderated their seven emotions (happiness, anger, sadness, joy, fear, terror and scare). He also installed officials embodying "Nine Virtues" to demonstrate good behavior to his people and promoted "Ten Doctrines", including the benevolence of a ruler, loyalty of a minister; love of a father, filial piety of a son; kindness of an elder brother, respectfulness of a younger brother; righteousness of a husband, obedience of a wife; gracefulness of elders and humbleness of young people. Moreover, he formulated a system of rites and music and governed the country by the rule of virtue.

After technologies for silkworm raising, silk-reeling, and weaving were developed by Huangdi's two concubines Leizu and Momu, the people were able to wear clothes made of silk. Huangdi also created Chuishang, a system of clothing to distinguish the officials' and ministers' positions by their robes, which could also present rituals to the world. He asked his officials Hucao and Boyu to make a dragon robe embroidered with the sun, moon, and stars, which represented heaven and dragon lines for only the emperor to wear in court. Renowned musician Linglun composed the song *Ode to the Dragon Robe* to praise Huangdi's achievements in governing the country by establishing the clothing system "Chuishang."

Linglun, a musician of the emperor, travelled to Xiegu Valley in Kunlun Mountain, west of Daxia, to pick the renowned bamboo that grew there for a flute to perform the sound of Huangzhong. Huangdi promoted music education, as music not only expresses people's emotions but also cultivates their hearts by manifesting their virtue, gratitude, and rewards, and expressing their feelings of peace and harmony.

Huangdi demanded his officials Cangjie and Jusong to create written characters after obtaining *The Picture of Dragon and Phoenix*, *Hetu* and *Luoshu* (a system of discerning time, direction, and seasons that people in ancient times used according to the stars). Cangjie was a historian. He collected pottery symbols, documents and paintings from many tribes after he came to the Youxiong

伶伦造笛
Linglun Making a Flute

为推算历法,用以纪年,黄帝带领大臣们前往具茨山迎日推筴,观测日月星辰的运行和节气的变化,用天干地支的组合来纪年,遂成黄帝历。

黄帝以圆坛祭天,方坛祭地,以明天地之道。又开祭先人之典,以兴国事。又行明堂之祭,山川祭祀。这种祭祀已成为法度之祀,礼之常制。

黄帝登上泰山,在山顶燃柴祭祀,又在山下祭祀三皇,然后在山下大会诸侯,不但了解到国家的具体情况,更重要的是国家的政策得以贯彻,礼仪、文字和农业技术得到了推广。为了寻求治国之策,他常带领大臣长途跋涉,翻山越岭,访贤问道。一天,黄帝乘车访道,当行至襄城郊野时迷了路。迟疑间,黄帝发现远处山丘上有一童子在放马,便下车缓步于前,问道:"此地是什么地方?"小童答:"襄城之野。""你知道具茨山在何处吗?""知道,就在北方百余里之地。"轩辕黄帝见

Kingdom, which greatly enriched the content of character formation. After years of research, Chinese characters finally came into being.

Instead of simply keeping tallies by tying knots in ropes, the characters created by Cangjie could be used to write articles, contracts, and documents. Xuanyuan adopted the characters to name every object and make decisions. Due to the creation of written characters, some superstitious witches were too scared to cheat people any longer.

For the sake of calendar calculation for marking years, Huangdi and the ministers went to Jucishan Mountain to greet the sun as a way of observing the motion of the sun, the moon and the stars as well as the change of solar terms. Therefore, the Huangdi calendar was created by using the lunar system of heaven and earth to record the years.

黄帝迎日峰
Huangdi Sun-Greeting Peak

To establish the principle of heaven and earth, Huangdi applied the circular altar to worship the heaven and the square altar to worship the earth. To bolster the affairs of the state, he created the ceremony of sacrificing to the ancestors. He also performed the sacrifice of Mingtang (a temple for important national events) and the sacrifice of mountains and rivers. These rituals evolved into the rituals of the law, which served as norms.

Climbing to the top of Taishan Mountain, Huangdi burned firewood to

牧童小小年纪竟知具茨山之名，甚为惊奇，又问："你知道具茨山有一位叫大隗的人吗？""知道，他是一个圣人，不但懂得天文地理，还精研《三洞经教》。"黄帝听罢，知道童子也是研道之人，急忙近前言道："你知道治理天下的道理吗？"童子答："治理天下跟牧马的道理一样，只要把害群之马除去就行了！"黄帝听后，急忙称天师而拜。

牧马童子
The Herd Boy

　　黄帝注重农业生产及人民生活，如实施农业灌溉、建立圃园、种桑养蚕、饲养家畜及纺纱、织帛、制衣、制陶、铸鼎和建造宫室、城邑、楼阁等，为社会发展打下了丰厚的物质基础。他也十分重视文字、绘画、雕塑、算术、诗歌、舞蹈、音乐、天文、历法、礼仪、祭祀及医药的发展，并取得丰硕成果。

　　黄帝爱民、亲民、惠民，大力发展农牧业、建筑业、手工业、交通业、商业，社会经济繁荣，人民安居乐业。

sacrifice. He then went downhill to worship the Three Sovereigns at the foot of the mountain, where he met with all the vassals to learn about the specific situation of the state, the implementation of the state policy, and the promotion of rituals, words, and agricultural technologies. He often led his ministers on long journeys over the mountains to visit wise people and ask for advice on strategies to govern the country. One day, Huangdi became lost in Xiangcheng on his way to ask about Taoism. While hesitating about the direction, he noticed a herd boy on a hill, so he dismounted and walked slowly to the boy, asking, "What is this place?" "The wilderness of Xiangcheng," the boy responded. Huangdi then asked, "Do you have any idea where Jucishan Mountain is?" "Of course, just over a hundred li (a unit of length, 500 meters) to the north," the boy replied. Huangdi was surprised that such a little boy would know about Jucishan Mountain and pursued asking, "Have you heard of a person named Dawei there?" The boy again replied, "Yes, he is a saint who not only masters astronomy and geography but also does elaborate research on *Sandong Jingjiao* (a classic of Taoism)." Knowing this, Huangdi realized that this boy was also a scholar of Taoism, so he asked, "Are you aware of the truth for governing the world?" "It is the same as herding horses, only to take out the black sheep," the boy responded. After listening to his words, Huangdi called him the Taoist master and worshiped him.

Huangdi paid great attention to agricultural production and people's livelihoods, including agricultural irrigation implementation, garden establishment, silkworm and livestock raising, spinning, silk weaving, cloth making, pottery, cauldron molding, and the construction of castles and cities. These interests laid a profound material foundation for social development. Huangdi also emphasized the creation and development of written characters, painting, sculpture, mathematics, poetry, dancing, music, astronomy, calendars, rituals, and sacrifice, as well as traditional medicine, which yielded fruitful results.

Huangdi cared about the people, remaining close to them and benefiting them. As a result of strong rapid development in agriculture, animal breeding, construction, handicrafts, transportation, and business, the social economy prospered, and people lived and worked happily.

The Xipo tribe was located at the foot of Jingshan Mountain, west of the Youxiong Kingdom. In Jingshan, there were many small furnaces for copper; from

荆山在有熊国西部，西坡部落就坐落在此山下。山中有许多炼铜的小窑炉，炉工把炼好的铜运到山下，再用大火炉把铜熔化后铸成各种器具。象征天、地、人的三个铜鼎已铸成，安放在场棚里。轩辕走近铜鼎，对岐伯说："鼎已铸成，这是师父的功德啊！"岐伯说："哪里是我的功德，明明是黄帝的隆德啊！"

河南灵宝铸鼎塬大殿
Cauldron-Molding Temple in Lingbao, Henan Province

轩辕黄帝去世后，黄帝的大臣左彻在轩辕丘改黄帝明堂为轩辕庙，用木雕成黄帝像，率大臣、诸侯国王祭祀黄帝。

《庄子》说："世之所高，莫若黄帝。"轩辕黄帝被后世尊奉为中华人文始祖。据宋代张君房《轩辕本纪》记述，轩辕黄帝在世111年。黄帝之后，帝颛顼、帝喾、帝尧、帝舜至夏、商、周三代，都尊黄帝为始祖，并继承黄帝的思想和伟业。秦汉以后，历朝历代的帝王都把黄帝当作人文始祖进行祭拜，并认同自己是黄帝的子孙。

these furnaces, the refined copper was transported downhill and melted in a large furnace before being cast into various utensils. Three bronze Dings (cauldrons), representing heaven, earth, and humanity, were cast and restored in the smelting plant. Approaching the bronze Dings, Xuanyuan said to Qibo, "The cast of the Ding is all your merits." Qibo replied, "It's not my merits but all your mercy, my lord."

After Xuanyuan Huangdi passed away, Zuoche, one of his ministers, renamed the Hall of the Yellow Emperor at Xuanyuan Hill as Xuanyuan Temple. There, Zuoche made a wood sculpture of Huangdi, to which he led other ministers and vassals to make sacrifices.

Zhuangzi said, "There is none higher in the world than Huangdi." According to the *Biography of Xuanyuan* by Zhang Junfang in the Song Dynasty, Xuanyuan Huangdi lived 111 years. Later generations named him the First Ancestor of Chinese civilization. He was respected as the First Ancestor by emperors from Zhuanxu, Ku, Yao and Shun to Xia, Shang, Zhou dynasties, who inherited his ideology and great causes. After the Qin and Han dynasties, every emperor sacrificed to Huangdi as the First Ancestor and identified themselves as Huangdi's descendants.

轩辕黄帝塑像
Statue of Xuanyuan Huangdi

第二章

黄帝治国方略

Chapter 2

Huangdi's Strategies of Governance

一、以人为本的执政理念

黄帝主张"天人合一",使人民理智地认识自然、认识社会、认识自己的生命和生活;黄帝开启了"人文思想",使人民致力于文化思维培育,从而使人文精神渐渐融入人的内心世界。

1. 黄帝铸三鼎,以象天地人

黄帝统一万邦,建都有熊,开启了远古中华文明的新时代,而这个文明的核心就是以人为本。以人为本来源于黄帝铸人鼎、建祖庙以祭祀祖先。

在中国,鼎的发现要追溯到8000年前的裴李岗文化。河南新郑是裴李岗文化的首掘地。遗址中发掘出了大量的石器和陶器。陶器中有陶钵、陶壶、陶鼎、陶碗。在当时,陶鼎是用来做饭的。后来,人们又以陶鼎作为祭器,以祭祀万神。在一鼎祭祀万神的时代,人类是以自然为本,在万神的护佑下进行生产与生活,人神保护的作用微乎其微,以人为本的观念也很微弱。而"黄帝作宝鼎三,象天、地、人",是一项建祖庙以重人道的重大事件。黄帝在河南灵宝铸鼎塬所铸的三鼎,一个是天鼎,用以祭天,祈求天降祥瑞,风调雨顺;一个是地鼎,用以祭地,祈求地献宝藏,五谷丰登;一个是人鼎,用以祭祖先,祈求祖先护佑,子孙繁衍。黄帝铸三鼎,是从一鼎祭万神的祭祀中把祭天、祭地、祭祖先独立出来进行,这种分别祭祀天神、地神、人神的行为标志着"天人合一""以人为本"的人文社会的正式到来。

以人为本的"人神"(祖庙)的单独确立,标志着人类在与自然做斗争的过程中产生了独特的价值观念,即"以人为本"的观念。先祖祭祀礼仪的奠定,为文明礼制的形成创造了条件。

人之本在于地,地之本在于天,天之本在于道,道之本在于自然,

I. People-Oriented Governing Philosophy

Huangdi advocated "harmony between man and nature," enabling people to understand nature, society, and their own lives and livelihoods in a rational manner. He initiated humanistic thought, leading people to devote themselves to the cultivation of cultural thinking, and gradually to integrate humanism into their inner world.

1. Molding Three Cauldrons to Symbolize Heaven, Earth, and Humanity

Huangdi unified all the Chinese states and made Youxiong the capital, starting a new era of ancient Chinese civilization. The core of this civilization was people-oriented, originating from Huangdi having one of the cauldrons discussed above molded for humans and building temples to worship ancestors.

In China, the discovery of cauldrons goes back 8,000 years to the Peiligang Culture. The first excavation site of this culture is Xinzheng in Henan Province, where numerous stone tools and pottery items were discovered. Among the pottery there were bowls, pots and cauldrons. In Peiligang Culture, pottery cauldrons were used to cook in, and later, as containers to offer sacrifices to all the gods. In this era, human activities were based on nature and considered under the protection of gods. Huangdi molding three cauldrons to symbolize heaven, earth and the human was a major event in developing an ancestral temple to value humanity. He molded three cauldrons at the Cauldron-Molding Plateau in Lingbao, Henan. The heaven cauldron was used to sacrifice to the sky to pray for auspiciousness and favorable wind and rain. The earth cauldron was for making sacrifices to the soil, for treasures and harvest. Lastly, the human cauldron was for sacrifices to the ancestors, for protection and blessings. In molding three cauldrons to sacrifice to the gods of heaven, earth, and humans separately, instead of one cauldron for sacrifices to all the gods, Huangdi marked the dawn of a people-oriented, humanistic society.

The notion of the human-centered "man-gods" (temples for ancestors) marked the emergence of unique human values in the struggle against nature, that is, the concept of "people-orientedness." The establishment of related rituals also

人与自然的和谐即是"天人合一"。黄帝合天道、守地道,重人道思想,其实质是"天道"与"人德"的辩证和依存,也是顺应天道自然的人之伦理。黄帝所言的"观天之道,执天之行""立天之道,以定人也",彰显出天人合一、人与自然的和谐观。它是建立在人对自然、人生、社会和精神层面认识基础上的,包括自然观、社会观、历史观、物质观、时空观、价值观。这些观念来源于人的生产和社会实践,并在改造自然和改造社会的实践中,形成了人与人之间的各种社会关系。黄帝受命于天,定位于地,成名于人,可见他是天人合一、以人为本思想的倡导者和实践者。其目标指向,一是天人和谐共处,二是整体社会利益,三是道德实践促进社会发展。

黄帝铸三鼎
Huangdi's Molding of Three Cauldrons

2. 垂衣裳而天下治

黄帝时代处于中原仰韶文化中后期。这一时期,人们仍然处在衣不蔽体的状态。为了尽快建立起社会新秩序,黄帝动员一切力量,栽植桑

gave birth to the formation of a civilized ritual system.

The root of man lies in the earth, that of earth in heaven, that of heaven in Tao, and that of Tao in nature. The harmony between man and nature is "the unity of heaven and human." Huangdi followed the way of heaven, complied with the way of earth, and valued the way of human. In its essence, this approach reflected the dialectical interdependence of "the way of heaven" and "human virtue," and demonstrated human ethics in line with nature. Huangdi's thoughts, such as "observing the way of heaven and to perform the acts of heaven" and "the way of heaven is established to determine human action," manifested the idea of unity between heaven and human, and harmony between man and nature. These notions were based on an understanding of nature, life, society, and spirituality, including the views of nature, society, history, matter, time and space, and values. They were derived from human production and social activities; in the transformation of nature and social practice, various social relations between people were formed. Appointed by heaven, settling on earth, and becoming well known among the people, Huangdi advocated and practiced his ideas about the unity of heaven and human, and put people first. His goals included the harmonious coexistence of heaven and the human, overall social interests, and a moral practice for social development.

2. Ruling by the Draping of Clothing

The Yellow Emperor era was in the middle and late period of YangShao Culture in the Central Plains. Before that period, people were still in a state of being dressed in rags. To establish a new social order as soon as possible, Huangdi mobilized all forces to plant mulberry trees, reel silkworms, and make clothes to dress the people. Leizu, the queen consort of the Yellow Emperor, invented technology to raise domestic silkworms, which promoted the development of silk weaving. Momu, his second consort, invented weaving technology and wove the silk into cloth. Hucao, one of Huangdi's ministers, cut the cloth and made it into garments. During Huangdi's time, agriculture was the primary industry and raising silkworms to make clothes was secondary. However, the latter had a pivotal position in the country's livelihood and solved the clothing problem. Huangdi ruled the country by dressing people. Hence, they had rules and were not as barbaric as

树，养蚕缫丝，织帛制衣，让人们都穿上了丝制的衣服。嫘祖是黄帝的元妃，发明了养蚕技术，野蚕家养又促进了蚕丝纺织业的发展。嫫母是黄帝的次妃，她发明了纺织技术，把蚕丝织成丝帛。胡曹将丝绸进行裁剪，做成了上衣。黄帝时期，农业是主业，养蚕制衣是副业。而蚕桑业在国计民生中有着举足轻重的地位，它主要解决了人民的穿衣问题。黄帝垂衣裳而天下治，是说人们从赤身裸体到穿上衣裳，都有了规矩，不像以前那么野蛮了，社会秩序好了，天下也得到了有效的治理。

黄帝不但创制出了衣服，而且衣服上还绣有图案，画日月星辰于衣上以象天，又染帛为五色，以表贵贱，区别等级或表示身份的不同。各级官员穿什么样的衣服，各种礼仪该穿什么样的服装，都有明确规定。黄帝所创制的衣冠制度不仅可以起到移风易俗的作用，而且也是为了建立社会新秩序，促进国家治理和社会文明进步。

3.创立婚姻制度

婚姻制度也是黄帝发明的。传说，黄帝与妻子嫘祖就是在中国农历六月六这天，在具茨山主峰风后岭八拜成婚的。八拜分别是拜天、地，拜日、月，拜山、河，拜父母和夫妻互拜。至今，新郑人民在每年的六月初六这天，都要在具茨山风后岭举行中华父母节，隆重纪念黄帝和嫘祖这两位中华民族始祖。

自从黄帝创立了婚姻制度，才有了真正意义上的家庭建立，使人类社会由野蛮、乱伦走向男女有别，各安其分，这是一种巨大的社会进步。黄帝时代的社会及家庭是十分和谐的。特别是当时的家庭中父与子、夫与妇、兄与弟之间所表现出的亲密与和谐关系，更说明婚姻与家庭制度的建立是国家和社会安定所需求的。普及婚姻家庭制度，对于构建新型的家庭关系，促进国家经济社会发展都有着重要的作用和意义。

before; society was in better order, and the country was effectively governed.

During the Yellow Emperor period, clothes were embroidered with patterns. Drawing the sun, the moon and stars on the clothes represented the sky, and dyeing the cloth in five respective colors indicated different social statuses. Officials at different levels were required to wear different kinds of clothes accordingly; on various ceremonies people should wear different kinds of clothes as well. The clothing system Huangdi invented not only played a role in changing the customs, but also helped to establish a new social order and promote national governance and social progress.

3. Establishing the Marriage System

Huangdi also invented the marriage system. According to legend, Huangdi and his queen consort, Leizu, were married on June 6 of the Chinese lunar calendar at Fenghouling Peak, the main peak of Jucishan Mountain. At their marriage ceremony, eight services were performed to heaven, earth, the sun, the moon, mountains, rivers, parents, and each other respectively. On the same day every year, the people in Xinzheng hold the Chinese Parents' Festival at the same place to commemorate the nation's two ancestors—Huangdi and Leizu.

中华父母节拜祖
Worshiping Ancestors on Chinese Parents' Festival

4. 爱民亲民惠民

黄帝是中国历史上爱民、亲民、惠民的典范。在黄帝的思想中，"以民为本"是核心内容。他在治国理政和一系列政策制定中，都紧紧围绕"以民为本"这个核心进行。要受民命治理好国家，他首先是紧紧依靠人民，做任何事情都必须符合人民的意愿，顺民意，得民心。他的以民为本的思想体现在诸多方面，如大力发展农业，实行井田制，使人民有田耕种；大力发展畜牧业，实行野畜家养，改善人民的饮食；大力发展手工业，烧制彩陶，缫丝织帛，丰富人民的生活；大力发展交通运输业，使人民出行有道，货运通畅；大力研究天文历法，使人民耕种不违其时；大力发展商业，使人民以物易物；大力发展礼乐，使人民遵从仁义道德。黄帝所做的一切都是上合天时，下合地利，中合民心的。

三足钵（仰韶）　　　　　　　　釜型鼎（仰韶）
Three-Legged Bowl (in Yangshao Culture)　Kettle-Type Cauldron (in Yangshao Culture)

5. 七年之治

黄帝的执政理念是以民为本。在国家建立之初，黄帝制定了七年发展计划。第一年，要遵从不同地域百姓的风俗习惯，这是为了顺应民心。第二年，要择用贤德之人为官吏，通过施爱于民以激励其奋勉。第三年，为了使民众过上富足的生活，废除了山泽之禁及贡赋。第四年，以德教育人民，按照严密的组织形式把人民组织起来，并挑选人才管理

Because Huangdi initiated the marriage system, nuclear families were established, transforming the society from barbarism and incest to the separation of men and women, making significant social progress. During the Yellow Emperor period, society and families were very harmonious. The intimate relationships between father and son, husband and wife, and brothers at that time evinced that the foundation of the systems of marriage and family were needed for the security of the country and society. The popularization of the system played an important role in building new family relationships and promoting the country's economic and social development.

4. Loving and Benefiting the People

Huangdi was a model of love and benefaction for the people in Chinese history. "Putting people first" was at the core of his ideology, and the development of his governance and policy was closely centered on the people. To govern the country well, he relied on the people and always acted in accordance with public opinion. His notion of putting people first was reflected in numerous aspects. For example, he developed agriculture by implementing the field system in a hash (#) pattern so that people could have fields to cultivate; he developed animal husbandry, raising wild animals at home to improve people's diet; he developed handicrafts,

小口尖底瓶（仰韶）
Small-Mouth Pointed-Bottom Bottle (in Yangshao Culture)

社会。第五年,用法律治理社会,并做到赏罚分明。第六年,百姓有了法律为准绳,廉耻观念就会形成。第七年,社会得到治理,人民便安居乐业,共享福祉。黄帝认为,遵从百姓的风俗习惯,是为了顺应民心;择用贤德之人施爱于民,是为了激励人民努力奋斗;要使民众有富足的生活,就要废除山泽之禁;要想有效地发号施令,就要把人民团结起来。国之本在于民,民之本在于土地,节民力以使,则财生。黄帝实行"井田制",按人口平均分配土地使用,其目的是"经土设井,以塞争端。立步制亩,以防不足……是以情性可得而亲,生产可得而均"。"井田制"始于黄帝,是黄帝的独创,从黄帝始,"五帝时代"至夏、商、周一直都在实行。

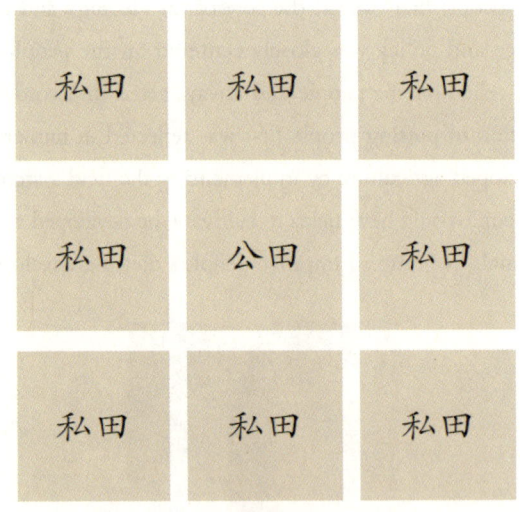

井田制
Field System in the Hash (#) Shape

6. 经济智慧

黄帝认为,经济好的表现,不仅仅在于衣食住行的满足,要使国家经济不断得到发展,就要紧紧把握整体经济的健康运行,既要国泰民安,也要社会祥和;既要兵强马壮,也要富足有余。必须持守中道,

making colored pottery, reeling silk and weaving cloth to enrich people's lives; he developed such transportation tools as boats and wagons so that people could travel more easily; he researched astronomy so that people could cultivate crops at the right time; he developed commerce so that people could exchange goods; and he developed rituals and music so that people could pursue morality. Everything that he did was in harmony with heaven, earth, and the people.

5. Seven-Year Governance

In the country's nascent stages, Huangdi made a seven-year development plan. In the first year, the customs and practices of people in different regions were to be followed to comply with their wishes. In the second, virtuous people were to be selected to be officials and encouraged to make people work hard by giving them love. In the third, the tribute and ban on hunting, fishing, ect. were to be abolished to enable people to live in abundance. In the fourth, the people were to be educated in virtues and tightly organized, and talented people were to be appointed to manage society. In the fifth, society was to be governed by laws, and rewards and punishments were to be given. In the sixth, with the laws as standards, the concept of integrity would be formed among the people. Finally, in the seventh year, society would be governed properly, and the people would live in peace and share the nation's welfare. Huangdi believed in the following principles: to follow customs and habits was to be in line with the people's wishes; to select virtuous people to give love to the people motivated them to strive hard; to abolish the ban on hunting, fishing, etc. enabled the people to have affluent lives; and to give orders effectively, it was needed to unite the people. To Huangdi, the essence of the country lied in the people and that of the people in the land. Huangdi implemented the field system in a hash shape to distribute the land equally according to the population, and to prevent disputes and promote affinities. This field system was initiated by Huangdi and followed from the Period of the Five Legendary Rulers (c. 2600 BC-c. 2070 BC) to the Xia, Shang and Zhou dynasties (c. 2070 BC -c. 771 BC).

6. Economic Wisdom

According to Huangdi, the indications of a good economy lay not only in

素位而行，保持国家经济始终处于良性运转和可持续发展。黄帝时代的农业、渔猎、畜牧、商业、手工业经济等都展现出物质文明的发展和壮大。黄帝时代的经济呈现出家庭私有形态，但就国家整体经济而言，它却是大同的、和谐的、发展的、繁荣的。

黄帝对当时的经济发展有五点主张：一是主张节俭，浪费就必然导致贫困；二是主张财富要积而为民所用；三是主张政府不干扰经济运行，也不放任市场自流；四是主张以德生财；五是主张合理经营，不欺不骗。这五点主张，既表现为以德为本的生财之道，又呈现出以诚信为本、和气生财的思想。这种思想落实为行动，大大促进了物质财富的积累，使经济社会得到繁荣发展。

7. 军事谋略

黄帝是一个伟大的军事家。他的军事思想核心是平定天下大乱，实现天下太平，"陶天下为一家"，建立大同社会和天下为公的和平、公正、祥和的社会新秩序。他站在政治的高度看待战争的不同性质，并充分肯定了代表人民利益的战争是正义的战争。他提出了"世兵道三""因时秉宜""以强执弱"的军事谋略，通过阴阳、动静、屈伸、强弱、卑高等矛盾对立转化关系，制定出正确、有效的军事战略方案，体现出其战略思想的伟大和完备。如："因时秉宜"论，说的是古代军事战争所应遵循的守则。黄帝主张，从战争动员、战争指挥到赢得战争胜利，每一个阶段、环节，都必须考察并顺应天时、地利、人力，否则就会失去根本，自取其祸。除此之外，还要准确、及时把握时机，当机立断，才能取得胜利。

the basic necessities of life being met, but also in the overall healthy running of the economy. It was necessary for the country to be peaceful and harmonious, as well as powerful and abundant. The people also needed to do their best to keep the economy developing smoothly. Agriculture, fishing and hunting, animal husbandry, commerce, and handicrafts in the Yellow Emperor's era revealed the development and growth of material civilization. While some private forms of economy existed, overall, the economy was public, harmonious, growing and prosperous.

Huangdi approached economic development according to the following five propositions. First, waste would inevitably lead to poverty. Second, wealth should be accumulated for and used by the people. Third, the government should neither interfere with the economic operations nor let the market run its course. Fourth, people should make money by being virtuous. Fifth, reasonable management should be encouraged, without deception or cheating. These five propositions were not only the virtue-based ways of earning money but also ways of managing businesses with honesty and in harmony. Put into practice, they greatly promoted the accumulation of wealth and social prosperity.

纺织
Textile

8. 开创中医

《黄帝内经》是中国最早的中医典籍，被称为"医家之宗"。它是黄帝与岐伯、雷公、少俞、伯高、少师等医家的医论记录，不仅记载有科学而系统的医学理论，丰富的防治疾病技术，还论述了天、地、人之间的相互关系以及人的生命规律，建立起中医学理论。《黄帝内经》涉及地理、养生学、哲学、天文学、心理学、季候、历法、阴阳、五行等各个门类。它是中国中医理论体系的源泉，是用阴阳五行学说解释人体与自然统一性的典范。

中原地区是中医药的发源地。在河南省新郑市具茨山主峰风后岭的山腰，有一座用石头建筑的房子，里边塑造有三位古代人物，三人呈坐姿，像是在讨论着什么。这座房子有个名字，叫医圣宫，是中国国家级文物保护单位轩辕庙所属建筑，里边塑造的三座塑像分别是黄帝、岐伯、雷公，传说这里就是中医奠基之作《黄帝内经》诞生的地方。

医圣宫
The Palace of Medical Sages

7. Military Strategies

Huangdi was a masterful military strategist. The core of his military approach was to pacify chaos and achieve peace, to "fuse into one nation," and to establish a new social order of peace, justice, and harmony. He viewed the different natures of wars from a political standpoint and fully affirmed that a war representing the people's interests was one of justice. He advanced military strategies, such as the principles of the world's military, appropriateness of the timing, and respecting the weak when being strong. Through the contradictory transformation of opposites, including yin and yang, strength and weakness, inferiority and superiority, Huangdi formulated a correct, effective military strategic plan, which reflected the excellence and completeness of his strategic thinking. The theory of "appropriateness of the timing," for example, focused on a principle that should have always been followed in ancient military warfare: at every stage of war, from mobilization to commanding to the end, timing, location, and human resources should be taken into consideration to avoid disasters. Huangdi also believed it was necessary to grasp opportunities and make the right decisions to achieve victory.

8. Pioneering in Traditional Chinese Medicine

Huangdi Neijing (*Huangdi's Internal Classic*) is the earliest Chinese medical achievement, known as "the origin of medicine," and is a record of the medical discussions of Huangdi and other medical men, such as Qibo, Leigong, Shaoyu, Bogao, and Shaoshi. It contains not only scientific and systematic theories and techniques for disease prevention and treatment, but also the rules of human life and descriptions of interrelationships between heaven, earth, and humanity. It also discusses geography, health science, philosophy, astronomy, psychology, yin and yang, the Five Elements and other disciplines. Hence, *Huangdi Neijing* is the source of the theoretical system of Chinese medicine and a model for explaining the unity of the human body and nature.

The Central Plains is the birthplace of Chinese medicine. On the hillside of Fenghouling Peak on Jucishan Mountain in Xinzheng, Henan Province, there is a house built of stone, occupied by three sculptures of ancient figures, seated as if in discussion. This house is named the Palace of Medical Sages and belongs to Xuanyuan Temple, a national cultural site for protection. The three figures are

溧水河（古姬水）
Yishui River (Ancient Jishui)

9. 保护生态

黄帝十分注重生态环境的保护。他认为行事没有准则，为天道所禁止；违背农事规律，为地道所禁止；背离教令，则为君主所禁止。对于地道的禁忌，他要求人们在修筑宫室时不要夷平山陵、填充沟壑、堵塞河流、破坏地理，不要滥兴土木、违反自然生态平衡。如果破坏了自然，就会危害人类自身。

portrayed as Huangdi, Qibo, and Leigong. Legend has it that this is the place where *Huangdi Neijing* was born.

9. Ecological Protection

Huangdi paid significant attention to the protection of the ecological environment. He believed that any action made without following specific guidelines would be forbidden by heaven, that violated laws of agriculture would forbidden by earth, and that deviated from the teachings would be forbidden by the monarch. Regarding prohibitions by the way of earth, Huangdi asked people not to raze mountains or hills, fill gullies or ravines, or block rivers when building palaces, as well as not to build indiscriminately or violate the natural ecological balance. If nature were destroyed, he knew it would endanger mankind itself.

洪堤
A Flood Protection Embankment

二、德法兼治的治国方略

黄帝的法制思想是黄帝将"道"与"法"完美结合而形成的思想。它揭示出"道"的规律性与"法"制建立的依据，以及"道"与"法"之间的相互关系，并提出了"以正治国"的合理主张。

1. 道与法的结合

黄帝统一天下，在有熊建国立都，开启了中国历史上最早的一个文化大发展时代。他紧密联系当时的社会实际，提出了"道生法"的科学理论。他将立法的依据、执守公正立法及法制的严肃性紧密结合起来，形成了法制理论与法制实践相结合的科学思想。他的"道生法"理论，不但揭示了法制建立的依据，而且在总体上说明了建立法制的重要性。"道"指宇宙万物的本原和普遍规律。黄帝将"道"称为"天时、地利、人事"，构成了"道"的总和。黄帝思想观念上的"法"，指的是法则和法度，而"道生法"是说社会的法度是依据宇宙世界的总规律而构建的。法制建立的目的，是维持社会秩序，法制实施的目的，是规范

德法兼治
Governing by Morality and Law

II. Governing by Morality and Law

Huangdi's conception of a legal system was a perfect combination of Tao and law. It revealed the regularity of Tao, the basis for the establishment of the law system, and the interrelationship between Tao and law. Huangdi also advanced the idea of "ruling the country by righteousness."

1. Combination of Tao and Legalism

Huangdi unified the nation and established the capital in Youxiong, initiating the earliest times of great cultural development in Chinese history. He put forward the theory of "Tao giving birth to law," which was based on contemporaneous social reality. He also combined the basis and enforcement of legislation with the seriousness of the legal system, and believed that the idea and practice of the legal system should align. His theory of "Tao giving birth to law" not only revealed the basis for but also explained the significance of establishing the legal system. Tao refers to the origin of all the things in the universe and universal laws. Huangdi regarded Tao as "timing, location, and people," and law as regulation rules. "Tao giving birth to law" meant that the law of a society was constructed according to the general law of the universe. The purpose of establishing the legal system was to maintain social order, and to implement the legal system was to regulate people's behaviors. Hence, Huangdi highlighted the centrality of the law system to a successful nation, which resulted in two aspects: on the one hand, the country was the core, emphasizing importance of legislative, executive, and judicial institutions; on the other hand, individuals were regarded as the starting point, stressing the idea of putting people first. Political awareness played a crucial role in the political civilization of Huangdi culture.

2. Governing by Morality

Huangdi's government by morality was characterized by the following features.

The first was harmony: Huangdi's rule always centered around the society's harmony. The governing system was known to the public, and the people's well-

人们的行为，突出了法治制度的中心地位。它不但以国家为核心，强调立法、行政、司法三大机构的重要性，而且以人为出发点，强调立足于人和以人为本，其政治意识和政治行为亦是黄帝文化政治文明的重要组成部分。

2. 道德政治

黄帝的道德政治有以下几个特点：

一是大同政治。黄帝理政始终围绕天下大同、天下为公展开，各项制度公开透明，政治目标指向始终是为着天下百姓的福祉和社会的祥和。

二是民主政治。无论国家官员，还是国内百姓，都可议论国事，提出批评建议。

三是清廉政治。黄帝提倡清廉节俭，爱惜民力民财，反对生活奢靡、贪污腐败。

黄帝为了防止贪污腐败蔓延，向各级官员提出约法六章。战国吕不韦《吕氏春秋·去私》中说："黄帝曰：声禁重，色禁重，衣禁重，香禁重，味禁重，室禁重。"这六禁重的"重"是"过分"之意。这句话意为各级官员在声乐、美色、服饰、饮食和居住方面要简约，反对奢靡、豪华、铺张浪费。

四是德法政治。黄帝以德依法治国，推行的各种法令均以德为准绳，以德法兼治为治国方略。

可以看出，黄帝时期的政治体系涉及的内容是广泛的，而这种广泛性归根结底则属于道德统领下的民主政治。道德统领政治，又表现为道德政治。道德政治的最终指向，是民主、民生、民权，以人为本的民主政治。

being and social peace were the political goals.

The second was democracy: both officials and ordinary people could discuss the country's affairs and present criticisms and suggestions.

The third was integrity: Huangdi advocated integrity, frugality, love for the people, economizing their money, and fighting against extravagant life styles and corruption.

In order to prevent the spread of corruption, Huangdi proposed six prohibitions to officials at all levels. *Mister Lü's Spring and Autumn Annals* written by Lü Buwei of the Warring States Period said, "Huangdi proposed prohibitions from lust when appreciating music, from obsession with women, from excessive concern for clothing, from intensive fragrance, from overt lush aliment and from extravagance in room decoration." The six prohibitions aimed to prevent officials from "excessive" behavior in six major aspects of life, and requested that officials at all levels should be simple in vocal music, beauty, garments, food and living, and oppose extravagance, luxury and wastefulness.

The fourth was governance by both morality and law: Huangdi ruled the country by implementing various laws and regulations on the basis of virtue.

社会祥和

Peace of the Society

3. 依法治国

黄帝的道法观是建立在道德伦理基础上的"以正治国"，就是要以道德为纲，"去私立公"，既要保护社会的公共利益，又要保护人民群众自身的利益。"去私立公"是黄帝政治思想的一个重要方面。

黄帝主张依法治理国家，不可妄为。如果不依法度而恣意妄为，则国可乱。如果依法办事，公正无私，赏罚分明，取信于民，则国可治，民可正。

道德和法律兼而并施，是黄帝以德依法治国的重要思想和伟大创举。以德依法治国，形成了以民主、法治为核心的政治制度。政治制度、政治意识、政治发展反映了黄帝对政治文明的探索和实践。

4. 治理国家的六种方法

黄帝在以德依法治国的前提下，提出了治理国家的六种方法，这就

《黄帝四经今注今译》
Present Notes and Interpretation of Huangdi's Four Classics

The political system of the Yellow Emperor period, therefore, involved a wide range of contents. The range ultimately aligned with democratic politics under moral domination, which, in turn, were manifested as moral politics, whose ultimate purpose was democracy, people's livelihood and rights, and people-oriented politics.

3. Governing by Law

Huangdi's theory of Tao and law meant that "the country should be ruled by righteousness" based on morality and ethics. "To rule by righteousness," the emperor should not focus on his own benefits but protect the public interests of society and the benefits of the people themselves. The concept of "rule by righteousness" was a key aspect of Huangdi's political thought.

Huangdi advocated the idea that the country should be governed by law. If the governors acted presumptuously without following the rules, the country would be chaotic. However, if the governors regulated the society in accordance with the rules, they could win the people's trust, maintain the country in good order, and encourage righteousness in the people.

The combination of morality and law was an important pioneering idea of the Yellow Emperor. Governing by both morality and law gave birth to a political system, with democracy and the rule by law as its core. The period's political system, awareness, and development reflected Huangdi's exploration and practice of political civilization.

4. Six Ways to Govern the Country

On the premise of governing by morality and law, Huangdi proposed the following six ways to rule the country, that is, the "six handles" mentioned in *Huangdi Sijing* (*Huangdi's Four Classics*). First, by examining minor changes, we can recognize the signs of a country's life or death. Second, by comprehensively analyzing objective factors, we can understand the reasons for the rise or fall of a country. Third, by moving with the times, we can defeat the powerful and revitalize the weak. Fourth, by governing by law, we can avoid confusion about the boundaries between right and wrong. Fifth, by adapting to changes properly, we can eliminate corruption and cultivate a new life. Sixth, by praising good deeds

是《黄帝四经·经法·<论>第六》所述的"六柄":一是观照几微,可知一个国家的生死之兆;二是综合辨析客观因素,就可以懂得一个国家存亡兴衰的原因;三是相时而动,就可以击败强大而振兴弱小;四是端正法度,就不会混淆是非的界限;五是应变不失,就能扫除腐败培植新生;六是尚善罚恶的使用交替变化,就能明德除害。这六种方法具备了,也就具备了应付一切的手段,国家便不会混乱而得以安定。黄帝从国家存亡兴衰的原因谈到怎样依法治国,从应对事件要因时而动谈到赏善罚恶、明德除害,可见黄帝治理国家的方略之精妙。黄帝关注历史发展规律以及治理国家的经验,为中国现代社会发展以及国家治理提供了历史参考。

and punishing evil ones, we can promote virtue and eliminate vice. Huangdi proposed these six methods to handle numerous affairs to make the country stable rather than chaotic. From the causes of the nation's rise and fall to the ways of governing by law, and from the need to respond to events according to the time to the necessity to promote virtue and eliminate vice, Huangdi's exquisite strategies for governing the country were comprehensively displayed. His concern for the laws of historical development and experience in governing the country provide historical references for the development of modern Chinese society and state governance.

三、和而不同的处世方法

中国早期文明之所以在许多地域先后发生，是因为这些地域中的文化相互作用和激发，故呈现出多样性的文化态势。

1. 融合与创新

黄帝时代，随着氏族社会的发展，黄河中下游地区的农业文化发展最为强劲，创造了当时最为瞩目的成就。这期间，以炎帝族为代表的西部文化，以蚩尤族为代表的东方文化和以轩辕族为代表的中原文化，经历了一次大碰撞。为了争夺生存空间，在中原形成了长期征伐的混乱局面。轩辕、榆罔、蚩尤为代表的三大联盟之间经过长期战争，轩辕联盟取得了最后胜利。轩辕黄帝建国立都中原有熊，开始了一系列政治改革，从根本上改变了当时氏族的文化格局和文化结构。

平息战争

Pacifying the War

III. Harmonious but Different Approaches to the World

Early Chinese civilization developed simultaneously in many regions due to the fact that the cultures in these regions interacted with and inspired each other. As a result, a diversity of cultural dynamics was formed.

1. Integration and Innovation

In the Yellow Emperor era, with the development of clan society, agriculture in the middle and lower reaches of the Yellow River developed best and achieved the most remarkable success. During this period, there was a significant collision among the western culture represented by the Yandi tribe, the eastern culture represented by the Chiyou tribe, and the Central Plains culture represented by the Xuanyuan tribe. The fight for survival space resulted in a chaotic situation of long conquests in the Central Plains. After a long period of war among the three alliances represented by Xuanyuan, Yuwang and Chiyou, the Xuanyuan Alliance was victorious. After establishing a unified country and building his capital in Youxiong, the Yellow Emperor Xuanyuan launched a series of political reforms and fundamentally changed the cultural patterns of the tribes.

Huangdi culture involves diversity. It was formed and accumulated through, first the integration of the cultures of the Central Plains, and, second the absorption of the cultures of the four directions. The cultures of the Central Plains referred to those created by the clans, tribes, ancient countries, and clan groups living in the Central Plains of China. The cultures of the four directions were those formed by the tribes and ancient countries around the Central Plains. Based on various cultures and combined with the needs of social development, Huangdi culture was achieved after bold reforms against old ideas, customs, and habits and a long period of innovation.

After the unification, Huangdi established administrative departments and settled the people. The attractiveness and influence of his political, economic, and cultural advantages led many ancient contemporary states to follow him. Chinese civilization "spread far and wide," and the surrounding states "came to show respect," which reflected the attractiveness of Huangdi's country and the

黄帝文化呈现出一体多样性。黄帝文化的产生和积累，一是对中原民族文化的吸收与融合，二是对四方文化的吸收和融合。中原文化是指生活在中国中原一带的氏族、部落、方国、古国和族团所创造的文化。四方文化，主要是指中原四周部族、古国的文化。黄帝文化，正是在吸收旧有的优秀文化的基础上，结合当时社会发展的需要，大胆改革以前的旧思想、旧风俗、旧习惯，并经过长时间的创新形成的。

轩辕黄帝统一万邦后，首先设立行政建制，划野分州，分封诸侯，安顿百姓。黄帝时期的政治、经济和文化优势所具有的吸引力和影响力，使得后来许多古国纷纷依附。华夏文明"四海远播"，周边国家"八方来朝"，体现的是中心国家的吸引力，表达的是华夏文明的向心力。黄帝的和平、善良、仁义、友爱等思想，归根结底来源于农耕文明的积淀。这种思想与这个民族的生存方式和发展方式有着最直接的关系。农耕文明的求稳定、求安定的内在趋向，形成了中华民族爱好和平的文化特征。

2. 陶天下为一家

中原地区是中华民族进入文明社会以来最重要的历史舞台，而轩辕黄帝则是这一文明舞台上的主角。中国是一个多民族的混合体，其文化"多样性"散布于全国各个地区，而"一体"则表现为多样性的综合。黄帝族和炎帝族是中华民族融合体中的两个主体民族。这两个主体民族的融合，包括民族文化的融合和血缘关系的融合，以及炎黄族周边其他民族的大融和。而这种融合，一是通过战争实现的，二是通过二者诸多的先进生产方式的不断融合实现的。这是黄帝统一万邦，"陶天下为一家"的过程和方式。此前炎帝族主要是稻作文化，而黄帝族的农耕文化指的是"艺五种"，即黍、稷、菽、麦、稻五种作物的种植。黄帝不断对生产技术进行革新，把炎帝族单纯的水稻种植发展为水旱并作，又发明了犁耕技术，形成了先进的农耕文化。

centripetal force of Chinese civilization. Huangdi's principles of peace, kindness, benevolence, and friendship originated from the evolution of agricultural civilization and directly influenced the survival and development of the nation. His tendency to seek stability resulted in the Chinese people's cultural characteristic of loving peace.

中华第一古都
The First Ancient Capital in China

2. Fusing into One Nation

The Central Plains were the most important historical stage of Chinese civilization, and Huangdi was the main character on that stage. China is a multi-ethnic nation, and its cultural diversity is manifested in all the country's regions while its "oneness" is displayed in a synthesis of its diversity. Huangdi's ethnic group and Yandi's were the two main groups in Chinese national integration, which involved the fusion of their cultures and blood relations and their integration with the other surrounding ethnic groups. The integration was achieved through wars and the continuous fusions of advanced modes of production. By this process, Huangdi unified the other states and "made the world

炎黄二族融合
Fusion of the Yan and Huang Tribes

　　黄帝王朝建立，结束了天下长期纷争的混乱局面。在黄帝王朝的统一管理下，各民族文化趋同的现象也成为一个主流。黄帝时分封了许多诸侯国，这些诸侯国思想上多趋同于国家的主流文化。黄帝王朝具有一个系统的管理机构，不仅要求人们遵守法律法规，还要求不同民族和地区的人们遵守制定的礼乐，使各民族的文化前所未有地、有效地、潜移默化地进行着交流融合。人们逐渐认同黄帝、认同国家，也认同大一统的华夏民族文化。

　　家国文化是轩辕黄帝所创造的独特文化。敬天地，尊祖先，是黄帝的人文情怀，同时也是早期中国文化的核心元素。它根植于华夏族民的内心世界，影响着华夏族民的思维方式和行为方式。黄帝创制了家庭制度、国家制度，形成了家国一体格局。这种社会结构为宗法思想的传播提供了丰厚土壤，使以家庭为细胞的农业型经济和血缘宗族关系得以永固。轩辕黄帝所构建的"大同社会"，使得早期中国广大地区的文化相互吸收、融会，最终形成了文化上的大融合。

one family." Previously, Yandi tribe's culture centered on rice, while the Huangdi tribe's farming culture involved "planting five kinds of crops," namely, broomcorn, millet, beans, wheat, and rice. By developing the Yandi tribe's rice cultivation and inventing plowing technology, Huangdi innovated production technology, forming an advanced farming culture.

The establishment of the Huangdi kingdom ended the long-standing chaotic strife, and various ethnic groups converged culturally under Huangdi's governance. During the Yellow Emperor's time, many states conformed to the mainstream culture of the country. The governing institutions required people of different ethnic groups and regions to comply with laws and regulations, as well as rituals. Hence, the cultures of various ethnic groups interacted and integrated subtly, effectively, and in an unprecedented way. Diverse peoples gradually identified with Huangdi, the nation, and the culture of a great unified country.

A combined family-nation culture was a unique culture created by the Yellow Emperor. Respect for heaven, earth, and ancestors was the humanistic sentiment of Huangdi, as well as the core element of early Chinese culture. It was rooted in the inner world of the Chinese people and influenced their ways of thinking and behavior. Huangdi created both the family system and the country system, treating the family and country as one. This social structure provided rich soil for the spread of patriarchal thought and perpetuated a family-based agricultural economy and blood clan relations. The harmonious society built by Huangdi made it possible for the cultures of ancient China to absorb and integrate with each other and eventually to form a great cultural combination.

四、以文化人的教化思想

黄帝时期的服饰制度和等级观念、礼乐制度下的和谐思想培育、道德教化下的善恶区别、中原与四方民族的思想融合、政治和文化上的认同、"九德之臣"的设立和"十义"道德规范的确立等,为社会文化的发展奠定了基础。因为这些文化具有现实社会的合理性,它不但对社会和谐有很大的促进力,而且对精神文明也具有巨大的促进作用。

1. 讲求诚信

黄帝所推行的"九行",主要讲的是"道德"二字。《黄帝内经》说:"天之在我者德也,地之在我者气也。"这是说"天人合一"就是"德人合一"。人完全按照德行行事,不违反自然规律,就与天德合一了。身心达到了完全遵守自然道德的境界,就是天人合一了。

具茨山山门
Gate of Jucishan Mountain

IV. Ideal of Educating People with Culture

During the Yellow Emperor period, social and cultural development was founded upon such cultures as the hierarchical costume system, cultivation of harmonious thought through rites and music, difference between good and evil under moral education, national thought fusion between the Central Plains and surrounding ethnic groups, political and cultural identity, establishment of "ministers with Nine Virtues," and the moral code of "Ten Doctrines." Due to their practical applicability to society, these cultures not only had a strong influence on social behavior, but also played a major role in promoting the cultivation of social and spiritual civilization.

礼乐教育
Rite and Music Education

黄帝怀有道德仁慈之心。为了天下苍生的福祉，他顺天时，观人运，谦恭自守，顺时而动，兼济天下，实为大德之人。黄帝的"利他"思想，是从本质上按照"利他"的要求，把"德"这种无形的财富形式变换为可触摸的有形的财富形式。黄帝的"利他"思想，不仅是德的一种表现，而且是道德思想的一种具体实践。

黄帝文化的本质属性是人文道德。黄帝文化是从自性道德中来，从修德、累德而来，从建功立业而来。

2. 九行十义

汉韩婴《韩诗外传》说："黄帝即位，施惠承天，一道修德，惟仁是行，宇内和平。"此述不但对黄帝以德治国思想做了高度概括，而且对国家所达到的文明程度也大加赞扬。"德"是黄帝文化的价值观和实践论，主要是从他以德治国来说的。"（黄帝）置四史以主图籍，使九行之士以统万国，九行者，孝、慈、文、信、言、忠、恭、勇、义。以观天地，以祠万灵，亦为九德之臣。"由此看来，九行也是九德。九德

|义行|勇行|恭行|忠行|言行|信行|文行|慈行|孝行|

九行
Nine Virtues

|幼顺|长惠|妇听|夫义|弟悌|兄良|子孝|父慈|臣忠|君仁|

十义
Ten Doctrines

1. Being Honest

The "Nine Virtues" that Huangdi promoted mainly focused on "morality." *Huangdi's Internal Classic* notes that "the virtues in heaven and the vitality from the earth are absorbed by me." This signifies that the "unity of man and nature" is the "unity of man and virtues." When a person acts in complete accordance with virtues without violating the laws of nature, he becomes one with the virtues of heaven. The unity of man and nature is achieved when the body and mind fully comply with natural morality.

Huangdi had a heart of moral kindness. He was a man of great virtue who followed the timing of heaven, observed the fortunes of people, remained humble and self-disciplined, and acted at the appropriate time to benefit the world for the welfare of society as a whole. His altruistic thought transformed morality from an intangible form of wealth into a tangible one. This altruistic thought is a manifestation of virtues and a concrete practice of moral thought.

Humanistic morality was the essential attribute of Huangdi culture, which was derived from natural morality, the pursuit and accumulation of morality, and the achievements of meritorious deeds.

2. Nine Virtues and Ten Doctrines

Hanshi Waizhuan (*Biography of Han Ying's Poetry*, poetry written in the Han Dynasty) states, "The Yellow Emperor acceded to the throne, benefited the people following the wishes of heaven, and emphasized morality and benevolence, so the universe was peaceful." This statement not only made an admiring generalization about Huangdi's principle of ruling the country by virtues, but also praised the country's degree of civilization. "Virtues" signify the values and practical theories of Huangdi culture drawn mainly from the emperor's practice of ruling the country by virtues. "Huangdi appointed four historiographers in charge of books and records and ordered people of 'Nine Virtues' to unify the whole country. 'Nine Virtues', that is, filial, kind, literary, trustworthy, remonstrative, loyal, respectful, courageous, and righteous, were employed to view heaven and earth and to sacrifice to all spirits." Hence, the "Nine Virtues" actually involved the practice of these nine virtues, reflecting the phenomenon that Huangdi both advocated virtues and practiced morality.

所反映出的是黄帝倡导德行的"气象",践行道德的"气象"。

黄帝以德治国,用人的根本在德,有德行的人心底才纯正,心灵纯正则行为端正,行为端正则社会和谐。黄帝对"九德"的提出,是他治国思想和道德实践的彰显。黄帝又提出了"十义",分别是君仁、臣忠、父慈、子孝、兄良、弟悌、夫义、妇听、长惠、幼顺。"十义"的提出和实施,对上下级关系的和谐、人与人之间关系的改善、家庭风尚的形成、社会的和谐发展起到了积极的促进作用。

In ruling the country by virtues, Huangdi believed in the essential role of virtues in engaging people in his vision for the nation. In his opinion, virtuous people were pure in heart and thus righteous in behavior, which led to social harmony. Huangdi's proposal of "Nine Virtues" is a manifestation of his governing ideology and moral practice. He also advanced "Ten Doctrines," for example, the benevolence of a ruler, loyalty of a minister; love of a father, filial piety of a son; kindness of an elder brother, respectfulness of a younger brother; righteousness of a husband, obedience of a wife; grace of elder people, and humbleness of younger people. The proposal and implementation of the "Ten Doctrines" played a positive role in promoting harmonious relationships between superiors and subordinates, improving interpersonal relationships, forming family customs, and giving rise to a harmonious society.

具茨山
Jucishan Mountain

五、黄帝的人文科学思想

1. 科技发明

黄帝注重各种技术的创造发明，如"黄帝经土设井，立步制亩""（黄帝）治五气，艺五种""黄帝命西陵氏劝蚕稼，月大火而浴种……因之广织，以给郊庙之服"。这些都是在农业生产方面的创造。在手工业生产方面，如机杼、衣服、布帛、冠、衮裘、染色、履、帐、幄、褥、毡、席、华盖、旗帜、扇；在冶炼铸造方面，有铜鼎、铜镜、刀、剑、戟、矛、戈、钟、货币；在建筑方面，如宫室、城邑、殿、楼、阁、台榭、堂、庙等；在交通方面，如舟、车、指南车、记里鼓等；在军事方面，如战鼓、军乐、号角、弓箭、烽火、蹴鞠、甲胄、盔、兵符、云梯、楼橹、战车等。另在医药、礼仪、民俗等许多领域均有诸多发明创造。

2. 创造文字

文字是人类用表意符号记录表达信息以传之久远的方式和工具。文字使人类进入有历史记录的文明社会。中国现存最早的成熟文字是公元前16世纪商代的甲骨文，至今已经有3600多年的历史了。而传说中，中国文字的发明与黄帝密切相关。至今，黄帝故里新郑还留存有一处古迹——仓颉造字台。传说它是黄帝的大臣仓颉发明文字的地方。

仓颉是黄帝的史官，黄帝统一万邦后，感到用结绳的方法记事，远远满足不了要求，就命他的史官仓颉造字。于是，仓颉就在当时的洧水河南岸一个高台上造屋住下来，专心致志地造起文字。可是，他苦思冥想，想了很长时间也没造出文字来。说来凑巧，有一天，仓颉正在静心思索，忽见飞来一只凤凰，凤凰嘴里叼着的一件东西掉了下来，正好掉在仓颉面前。仓颉拾起来，看到上面有一个蹄印，可仓颉辨认不出是什

V. Huangdi's Thought of Humanistic Science

1. Scientific and Technological Inventions

Huangdi paid attention to the creation and invention of technologies. He created the nine-square field system with one large square divided into nine small ones (like the Chinese character 井), measured, and distributed the field by pacing; he studied the festivals and seasons and planted all kinds of crops; he ordered the Xiling clan to persuade people to raise silkworms, bathe the silkworm breeds in February, therefore, more clothes were woven for the worship in the suburban temple. These are all innovations in agricultural production. In handicraft production, there is evidence of looms, cloth, silk, crowns, leather, dyeing, shoes, tent weaving, mattresses, felt, mats, canopies, banners, and fan. In smelting and casting, there are bronze cauldrons, bronze mirrors, knives, swords, halberds, spears, gongs, bells and coins. In architecture, there are palaces, cities, halls, towers, pavilions, terraces, halls, and temples. In transportation, there are boats, wagons, south-pointing carts, and mileage-counting drums. In military items, there are drums, musical works, horns, bows and arrows, beacon fire, Cuju, pieces of armor, helmets, commander's seals, ladders, wooden watchtowers, and chariots. Many

创造发明
Creation and Invention

么野兽的蹄印，这时正巧走来一个猎人。猎人看了看说，这是貔貅的蹄印，与别的兽类蹄印不一样，别的野兽蹄印他一看就知道。仓颉听了猎人的话很受启发。他想，万事万物都有自己的特征，如能抓住事物的特征，画出图像，大家都能认识，这不就是字吗?

仓颉造字台
The Platform for Cangjie's Creating Characters

仓颉鸟迹寿纹
Cangjie's Pattern of Longevity with Bird Calligraphy

从此，仓颉便注意仔细观察各种事物的特征，如日、月、星、云、山、河、湖、海，各种飞禽走兽和日常应用器物，并按其特征画出图形，造出许多象形字来。这样日积月累，时间长了，仓颉造的字也就多了。仓颉把他造的这些象形字献给黄帝，黄帝非常高兴，立即召集大臣，让仓颉把造的这些字传授给他们，于是，这些象形字便开始应用起来。为了纪念仓颉造字之功，后人把河南新郑市仓颉造字的地方称作"凤凰衔书台"，公元10世纪宋朝时还在这里建了一座寺庙，取名"凤台寺"。

其实，仓颉是根据他多年来所采集的龟甲、陶器、图画、具茨山岩

other inventions and creations exist in other fields, including medicine, etiquette, and folk customs.

2. Creation of Chinese Characters

Characters are an old means and tool for human beings to record and express information in ideographic symbols to pass them down through generations. The written word has enabled mankind to develop civilized societies with recorded histories. The earliest surviving mature script in China is the oracle bone script of the Shang Dynasty in the 16th century B.C., which indicates that Chinese characters have a history of over 3,600 years. Legend has it that the invention of Chinese characters is closely related to the Yellow Emperor. To this day, there is a historic site—the Platform for Cangjie's Creating Characters in Xinzheng, hometown of the Yellow Emperor—where Cangjie is said to have created characters.

Cangjie was the official historian of the Yellow Emperor. After unifying China, Huangdi felt that keeping records by tying knots was inadequate to meet the needs of the growing civilization. Thus, he ordered Cangjie to create characters. Therefore, Cangjie settled down in a house built on a high platform on the south bank of Weishui River and concentrated on creating characters. He thought hard for a long time but failed to produce anything. One day, as Cangjie was meditating, he suddenly saw a phoenix flying in the sky; it held something in its mouth, which fell down right in front of him. Cangjie picked it up and noticed a hoofprint on it. As he was wondering what kind of wild animal the print came from, a hunter happened to pass by, looking at it, and said, "It is the hoofprint of pixiu (a mythical wild animal), which is different from one of other beasts. I can tell the hoofprints of other beasts at a glance." Inspired by the hunter's words, Cangjie realized that everything had its own feature. If the features were memorized and drawn with pictures, everyone could recognize them. Were they not characters?

From then on, Cangjie carefully observed the features of various things, such as the sun, the moon, stars, clouds, mountains, rivers, lakes, seas, birds, animals, and everyday artifacts. According to the items' features, graphics were drawn to create pictographs. In this way, over a long period, Cangjie made more characters.

画符号，通过长时间研究才创造出文字的。相传，他经常登上具茨山踏察岩画，看到不同类型的岩刻上千处。有类似河图洛书、星象图、太阳花的，还有岩石上磨刻着圆穴、方穴、方格、网格、沟槽、曲线、植物和人物符号的。仓颉根据岩画符号的特征，按圆形、方形、线形、菱形分为四类，计百余个字符，供造字时参考。如：用圆表日，半圆表月，方格表田，凹穴表丁等。他把具茨山岩画符号作为母体，大大丰富了造字的内容。为了创造可通用的文字，仓颉年复一年、日复一日地反复研究、整理岩画符号，终于创造出了文字。

仓颉造出字后，文字在黄帝王朝各项制度的颁布中起到了重要的作

具茨山岩画
Rock Paintings in Jucishan Mountain

He presented them to the Yellow Emperor, who was overjoyed and immediately called his ministers together, and asked Cangjie to teach them. Thus, these pictographs were put to use. To commemorate the achievements of Cangjie, later generations called the site where Cangjie created the characters the "Terrace of Phoenix Picking Up the Imperial Edict." In the Song Dynasty, in the 10th century, a temple was built there, named Fengtai Temple.

As a result of long-term research, Cangjie created the characters according to the tortoise shells, pottery, pictures and rock painting symbols in Jucishan Mountain he had collected over the years. Legend goes that he often went up to Jucishan Mountain to inspect the rock paintings and saw thousands of different types of rock carvings. There are those similar to Hetu and Luoshu, star maps and sunflowers, as well as those with round holes, square holes, squares, grids, grooves, curves, plants and figures carved on rocks. According to the characteristics of the rock painting symbols, Cangjie divided them into four categories, including round, square, linear and diamond shapes, and came up with more than one hundred symbols for reference in creating characters, for example, a round shape indicating

具茨山岩画符号
Rock Painting Symbols in Jucishan Mountain

用，有力地推动了社会的文明和进步。不难看出，文字的发展和成熟是一个不断孕育、积累和演化的过程，是循着人类进步的历史进程逐渐发展和成熟的。

3. 文化艺术

黄帝时代的文化教育是通过多种形式进行的。通过教育，社会文艺得到巨大发展。如诗歌《断竹》就是一例。南朝梁代人刘勰的《文心雕龙》说："黄歌《断竹》，质之至也。"又说："寻二言肇于黄世，《竹弹》之谣是也。"歌辞曰：

断竹，续竹。

飞土，逐肉。

这首《弹歌》选自《吴越春秋》。据记载，春秋末年越国的国君勾践向楚国的射箭能手陈音询问弓弹的原理，陈音在回答时引用了这首民歌。后人将歌辞记录了下来。

远古时代的黄歌《断竹》，即《弹歌》，在今人看来，属于诗歌一类，被称为"二言之始"。当时诗歌的产生，一是出于人类的天性，因为人类具有模仿的天性；二是当时社会生活的真实写照。"断竹，续竹"，是歌咏"弹弓"的生产制作过程，就是先把竹竿截断，然后用弦将截断的竹竿两头连接起来，制成弯弓，这样，"弹弓"就制作完成了。而"飞土，逐肉"，就是猎手用弹弓将泥丸射出，击伤鸟兽之类的猎物。这首诗歌既表现出当时族民的聪明智慧，同时也表明了当时社会的进步。此诗虽简短，但诗句整齐，内容质朴，表现出诗歌的真实与历史的真实。

《云门》为轩辕氏乐歌，至后世乐与辞尽亡，仅留其名。唐代元结出于复古的考虑，凭己意补足了歌辞：

玄云溶溶兮，垂雨濛濛。

类我圣泽兮，涵濡不穷。

the sun, a semicircle the moon, a square the field, and a concave a new baby born into the family. He took the rock painting symbols in Jucishan Mountain as the matrix, which greatly enriched the content of Chinese characters. In order to create universal characters, Cangjie studied and sorted the characters repeatedly day after day for years, and finally created the characters.

After Cangjie created characters, they played an important role in the promulgation of various systems of the Yellow Emperor era. It is not difficult to see that the development and maturity of characters is a process of constant gestation, accumulation, and evolution, following the historical process of human progress.

3. Culture and Art

Cultural education in the Yellow Emperor era was carried out in various ways. Through education, social literature and art developed substantially, as exemplified by the poem *Broken Bamboo*. *Wenxin Diaolong* (a comprehensive work on literary theory written by Liu Xie in the Liang era of the Southern Dynasty) notes, "The poem *Broken Bamboo* of the Yellow Emperor period is of the highest quality." The text further states, two-character poems stemmed from that period, and one example is the ballad of *Bamboo Slingshot*, which says,

Break bamboo, make bow.

Eject clod, shoot prey.

This poem was selected from *Wuyue Chunqiu* (*Spring and Autumn Annals of States Wu and Yue*). It was recorded that at the end of the Spring and Autumn Period, Gou Jian, the ruler of the State of Yue, asked Chen Yin, an expert archer of the State of Chu, about the principle of bow shooting. Chen Yin quoted the folk ballad above in his reply, which was recorded by later generations.

The ancient poem *Broken Bamboo* was a song about a slingshot. To modern critics, it belongs to a kind of poetry known as early "two-word poems." At that time, poems were born of human nature because humans had the nature of imitation and were true portrayals of social life. "Break bamboo and make bow" describes the process of making a slingshot, which is to cut the bamboo and connect the two ends of the broken bamboo with strings to make a curved bow.

黄云漠漠兮,含映逾光。

邈我圣德兮,溥被无方。

黄帝时期音乐的发展进入兴盛期,据文献记载,各种乐器大量出现,如瑟、琴、竽、笙、簧、笛、钟、钲、铙、角、磬、鼓、律管等,当时已制有五音十二乐律。黄帝作五声是为了政五钟,立五行以正天时,置五行官以正人位。黄帝时不仅有乐曲,而且有乐歌,创作的音乐有《云门》《清角》《咸池》《大卷》等。音乐的作用,是悦人之心。

《云门》乐舞
Dance of *Cloud Gate* Accompanied by Music

关于黄帝时的军乐,宋张君房《轩辕本纪》说:"帝以伐叛之功,始令岐伯作车(军)乐鼓吹,谓之箫铙之歌,以为军之警卫,《棡鼓曲》《灵夔吼》《雕鹗争》《石坠崖》《壮士怒》《玄云》《朱鹭》等曲,所以扬武德也,谓之凯歌。"《日下旧闻考》说:"黄帝出师涿鹿,以棡鼓为警卫,其曲有十:一曰《震雷惊》,二曰《猛虎骇》,三曰《鸷鸟击》,四曰《龙媒蹀》,五曰《灵夔吼》,六曰《雕鹗争》,

In this way, the slingshot is finished. "Eject clod and shoot prey" signifies that the hunter ejects clod from the slingshot to shoot the prey. The poem, therefore, reflects the wisdom of the clans and social progress. Although the poem is brief, its lines are neat, and its content is plain, illustrating the reality of poetry and history.

The music and lyrics of *Cloud Gate,* a song of the Xuanyuan clan, were both lost in the later generations, leaving only the name. In the Tang Dynasty, Yuan Jie, wishing to restore the song's original music, supplemented the lyrics of the song with his own meaning:

Dark clouds are flowing, the rain drizzling,

As my holy kindness contains endless moisture.

The clouds are indistinct but reflect light,

Just as my holy virtue has no ending.

Music prospered during the reign of the Yellow Emperor. According to literary records, various musical instruments appeared in large numbers, for example, zithers, flutes, reeds, bell, percussion instruments, cymbals, horns, chimes, and pitch pipes, which could create five musical tones and twelve temperaments. Huangdi made the five tones to regularize the five bells, established the five elements—gold, wood, water, fire, and earth—to regularize the seasons, and installed five officials to regularize their positions. At that time, there was not only musical composition but also song accompanied by music, for example, *Cloud Gate*, *Clear Horn*, *Salt Pond*, and *Great Scroll*. The role of music is to please people's hearts.

Regarding military music in the Yellow Emperor era, *Xuanyuan Benji* (*Biography of Xuanyuan*) written by Zhang Junfang of the Song Dynasty observes, "To celebrate the victory of fighting against the rebels, the emperor ordered Qibo to make chariot (army) music, also called the ballad of flute and cymbal, to alert and guard the army. Then, such songs as *Oak Drum Tune*, *Roar of Mythical Creature Kui*, *Battle of Eagle and Osprey*, *Rock Falling off a Cliff*, *Wrath of the Warrior*, *Dark Clouds*, and *Ibis* were written to promote military virtues, being thus regarded as ballads of victory." *Present Study of Old News* notes that Huangdi set out to Zhuolu, employing oak drums as guards, involving ten songs: *Thundering Shock*, *Fierce Tiger Terror*, *Bird of Prey Strike*, *Dragon

七曰《壮士奇志》,八曰《熊罴哮吼》,九曰《石荡崖》,十曰《波荡壑》。并皆有辞,今亡考矣。"黄帝时代作军乐的目的,一是扬德建武,二是鼓舞兵士斗志,三是震慑敌方,四是庆贺胜利。

黄帝时代是舞乐并兴的时代。舞乐艺术在考古学上也有发现,如青海马家窑文化的舞乐彩陶盆上,绘有三组舞者图像,可证舞乐、绘画艺术在中国是自古存在的。

黄帝时代艺术的产生来源于社会意识,包括人们的理想追求、情感习惯、道德风尚和审美情趣等。而这种艺术的创造,又具有民族性。

黄帝文化,从总体来说,对于人的塑造、人的全面发展具有极大的促进作用。它既有认识和传播功能,又有教化和凝聚功能。更重要的是,它具有文化社会的调适和控制功能,又有规范人的行为,维护社会道德,维持社会安全,促进社会平衡发展的功能。

Tread, *Roar of Mythical Creature Kui*, *Battle of Eagle and Osprey*, *Lofty Ideal of the Warrior*, *Roar of Bears*, *Rock Falling off a Cliff*, and *Waves Washing Through the Gully*. All these songs had lyrics that are now lost. The purposes of military music were to promote morality and build military force, boost soldiers' morale, deter the enemy, and celebrate victory.

The Yellow Emperor era was characterized by a combination of dance and music, as evinced by archaeology. For example, three groups of dancers are painted on a colored pottery basin from the Majiayao culture of Qinghai Province. It can thus be proved that dance, music and painting existed in ancient China.

马家窑出土的彩陶盆
Colored Pottery Basin Unearthed in Majiayao

The creation of art in the Yellow Emperor era arose from social consciousness, including people's ideal pursuits, emotional habits, moral fashions and aesthetic tastes. The creation of art was a national trait.

On the whole, Huangdi culture plays an important role in promoting the shaping and all-round development of human beings. It has the functions of cognition and communication, of enlightenment and cohesion. More importantly, it promotes cultural and social adjustment and control, regulates human behavior, and maintains social morality, security, and balanced development.

第三章

黄帝文化传承

Chapter 3

Inheritance of Huangdi Culture

黄帝文化是中华民族的精神血脉，它所蕴涵的人生智慧、价值观念、道德理想以及对世界的感知方式，为中华民族提供了丰富的精神文化滋养。黄帝文化经历了五千多年的历史积淀，不断凝结、升华而培育了伟大的民族精神，形成了强大的民族凝聚力、创造力、生命力。黄帝文化的发展是一个历史连续体，从过去延续到现在，也必然从现在延续到未来。

一、黄帝文化在中国历史上的影响

1. 各种方式传播

黄帝文化的传承一般有四种情况。一是官方典籍，即历朝历代国史所记载的黄帝事迹。二是民间故事，即民间口头相传的黄帝故事。三是神话传说，即汉代以降在方士著作中或民间的传说。四是后世研究，即历代所编书籍。黄帝文化之所以能得以传播，是因为作为人文始祖的黄帝，为人类社会发展做出了重大贡献，其影响深刻，其思想和功绩流传下来，被后人弘扬。

夏、商、周时代，黄帝文化得到进一步发展，已成为当时民族意识和民族文化发展的精神支柱。春秋战国时期，有关黄帝的传说多有记载，其传说更侧重于黄帝的功绩和人文方面，对当时的社会发展起到了重要的推动作用。这一时期，诸子蜂起，百家争鸣，逐渐形成了古代中国文化思想的大融合。秦代，黄帝文化促进了民族的统一和发展，具有划时代意义。汉初，推行黄老之术，实行无为而治，国力得到迅速恢复。

汉武帝时期，儒家学说确立了至尊地位，黄帝文化得到继承和发展，黄帝的传说也开始兴盛起来。传说的内容主要是黄帝的出生地和居住地、功绩等。汉代司马迁在《史记》开篇首列《五帝本纪》，将黄帝列为五帝之首。《左传》《逸周书》《管子》《山海经》《大戴礼记》

Huangdi culture is the spiritual bloodline of the Chinese nation. The wisdom of life, values, moral ideals and the perception of the world this culture embodies provide rich spiritual and cultural nourishment for China. Through more than 5,000 years of historical accumulation, this culture has continuously condensed, sublimated, and nurtured a great national spirit, forming strong national cohesion, creativity, and vitality. Its development is a historical continuum, extending from the past to the present and, inevitably, to the future.

Ⅰ. Influence of Huangdi Culture in Chinese History

1. Spread in Various Ways

There are generally four means of inheriting Huangdi culture. The first is through official books, in which Huangdi's deeds are recorded in the national histories of successive dynasties. The second is through the folk stories passed down orally. The third is through myths and legends, namely, local works or folk legends after the Han Dynasty. The fourth is through the study made in later generations, such as the books compiled in the following dynasties. There are several reasons for the spread of Huangdi culture. As the first ancestor of Chinese civilization, Huangdi contributed greatly to and profoundly influenced the development of human society. His thoughts and achievements have been handed down to and carried forward by later generations.

In the Xia, Shang and Zhou dynasties, the culture was further developed and became the spiritual pillar for the development of national consciousness and culture in those periods. During the Spring and Autumn Period and the Warring States Period, many legends circulated about Huangdi, which focused particularly on his achievements and humanistic interests, and played an important role in promoting the social development. In those periods, the rise of various schools of thought gradually led to a major integration of ancient Chinese culture and thought. In the Qin Dynasty, Huangdi culture promoted the unity and development of the nation, which was of epoch-making significance. At the beginning of the Han Dynasty, the doctrines of Huangdi and Laozi were enacted and the country's national strength was quickly recovered.

During the reign of Emperor Wu of the Han Dynasty, Confucianism

《淮南子》等书籍，也不同程度地记述了轩辕黄帝的伟大功绩。

《史记》
Records of the Grand Historian

至今，黄帝文化的传播一直没有中断过。这是因为：第一，轩辕黄帝是中国的奠基者，中华民族的缔造者，其思想一直被继承了下来。第二，黄帝时期有一系列创造发明，涉及农工渔牧、衣食住行、文字礼乐、时令节候，这些创造发明造福人民，万世为用。第三，黄帝时期奠定的国家制度，在各个朝代都得到了一定的继承和发展。第四，历朝历代重视血缘关系和祖先崇拜，黄帝作为中华民族的主要血缘始祖，被历代人民祭拜。第五，由于轩辕黄帝的民族融合思想不断发展壮大，黄帝文化的融合力、凝聚力、向心力进一步加强。时至今日，黄帝文化的影响力不但没有淡化，反而更加强大。这也是中华文明五千多年绵延至今，从未中断的基因密码。

2. 尊黄帝思潮的兴起

在中国历史上，曾出现过四次尊黄帝思潮。第一次是在战国时期，这一时期诸子百家均言黄帝，如《世本》《竹书纪年》，还有《国语》都记有"五帝"系统，黄帝已被尊称为华夏族的祖先。第二次是西汉时期，由于秦末汉初的战乱，统治者奉行"黄老之学"。到了汉武帝时，

established its supremacy, and Huangdi culture was inherited and developed, allowing legends about Huangdi to flourish. The legends are mainly about the places of Huangdi's birth and residence, as well as his merits. In the Han Dynasty, Sima Qian listed him as the first of the Five Legendary Rulers at the beginning of *Records of the Grand Historian*. Other books, such as *Zuo Zhuan* (*Zuo's Commentary to the Spring and Autumn Annals*), *Yizhoushu* (*The Book of the Zhou Dynasty*), *Guanzi* (a compilation of the various schools of thought in the pre-Qin period), *Shanhai Jing* (*Classic of Mountains and Seas*), *Dadai Liji* (a book on the rites of Dadai in the Han Dynasty), and *Huainanzi* (a philosophical work from the Western Han Dynasty), also describe his achievements.

To this day, the spread of Huangdi culture has been uninterrupted for the following reasons. First, Huangdi was the founder of China and the creator of the Chinese nation. His ideology and legacy have been inherited. Second, a series of inventions occurred during his period, including in agriculture, industry, fishing, and animal husbandry, food, clothing, housing, and transportation, writing, rites and music, and seasonal festivals, which benefited the people and will continue to be used. Third, the state system that was established then was inherited and developed to a certain extent by different dynasties. Fourth, successive dynasties attached great importance to blood relationships and ancestor worship, and as the main blood ancestor of the Chinese nation, Huangdi has been worshiped by people of all generations. Fifth, due to the continuous development and expansion of his concepts of national fusion, China's integration, cohesion, and centripetal force have been further strengthened. Today, the influence of Huangdi culture is not weakened, but strengthened. It is also the uninterrupted genetic code of Chinese civilization, which has lasted for more than 5,000 years.

2. Rise of Honoring Huangdi

In Chinese history, there were four waves of thought honoring the Yellow Emperor. The first took place in the Warring States Period when he was mentioned by hundreds of scholars, such as the records in *Shi Ben* (*Origin of Genealogy*), *Zhushu Jinian* (*Chronicle Written on the Bamboo Slips*), and *Guo Yu* (*Discourses of the States*), which recorded the chronology of the Five Legendary Rulers. In these texts, Huangdi is honored as the ancestor of the

不仅推行罢黜百家、独尊儒术的政策，而且极力推崇黄帝，从而形成了中国历史上的第二次尊黄帝思潮。

中国历史上第三次尊黄帝思潮，是在明末清初形成的，它对近代民族主义思想的形成和发展起到了十分重要的促进作用。

明末清初王夫之（别称船山）的《黄书》，对黄帝的功绩和品德给予了很高的评价。他还特别称颂黄帝的道德，即所谓的"黄中"。在《黄书》的"后序"中，他说："述古继天而王者，本轩辕之治，建黄中，拒闲气殊类之灾，扶长中夏以尽其材，治道该矣。"船山学社现任社长王兴国说："可见，黄中讲的是一种内在的美德，有了它，就可以抗拒异民族所造成的灾难，扶植中土人士充分地展示其才华，从而达到完备的治道。这种黄中美德也就是汉民族的民族正气。"《黄书》中，船山充分肯定了黄帝在中国历史上的重要地位，并说黄帝建中央王国，各诸侯国均能听命于黄帝，拥戴其正朔，数千年之间社会始终保持着和平和谐的状态。但到了秦、汉以后，国家"合极而乱，乱极而离，离极而又合"。他所编《黄书》的目的，就是要"矫起所自失，以返轩辕之区画"，希望统治者能够通过反思，矫正自己的失误，实现轩辕黄帝所

王夫之像
Portrait of Wang Fuzhi

Chinese nation. The second wave was in the Western Han Dynasty. Due to the wars in the late Qin and early Han dynasties, the rulers adopted "the doctrines of Huangdi and Laozi." Emperor Wu of the Han Dynasty not only carried out the policy of subjugating all schools of thought and honoring Confucianism only, but also highly praised Huangdi, which led to the second wave of thought in Chinese history.

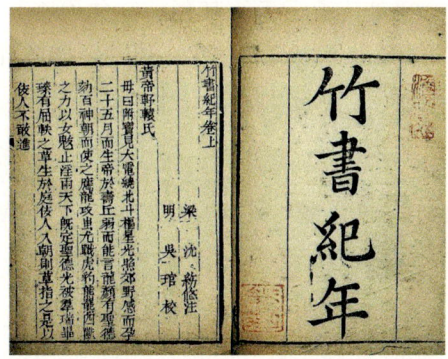

《竹书纪年》

Zhushu Jinian (Chronicle Written on the Bamboo Slips)

The third wave came into being at the end of the Ming Dynasty and the beginning of the Qing Dynasty, which played a very important role in promoting the formation and development of modern nationalism.

Huangshu, a book written by Wang Fuzhi (also known as Chuanshan) in the late Ming and early Qing dynasties, praised Huangdi highly for his great achievements. Wang Fuzhi also paid special tribute to Huangdi's morality, known as the virtue of the Yellow Emperor. In the epilogue of *Huangshu*, Wang Fuzhi stated, "Huangdi was selected as a king, and his governance was promoted. He built the virtues, resisted the disasters from other ethnicities, and helped the Chinese nation to display talents." Wang Xingguo, present president of the Chuanshan Learned Society has said, "It can be seen that the virtues of the Yellow Emperor are inner, which can resist the disasters caused by the foreign nations and help the Chinese people to fully display their talents to achieve complete governance. This virtue is just the national righteousness of the Han nation." In *Huangshu*, Wang Fuzhi fully affirmed the crucial position of Huangdi

谋划的和谐社会。

第四次是清代末年，民族主义思想兴起，辛亥志士将《黄书》视为民主革命的旗帜，掀起了尊黄帝高潮。当时最重要的代表人物是章太炎，他极力推崇《黄书》。1901年，章太炎直接引用《黄书》中的重要言论，以宣传其民族主义思想。1902年，他在《訄书·原人篇》中说："观于《黄书》，知吾民之皆出于轩辕。"在清末对《黄书》的推崇中，他起到了引领潮流的作用。1903年，黄藻以撰述者为"黄帝子孙之多数人"，编辑者则为"黄帝子孙之一个人"的标注编辑出版了《黄帝魂》一书。初版时书中收入文章29篇，1911年再版时增至44篇。此书采用黄帝纪年，扉页刊印黄帝像，在像的上方标有"世界第一之民族主义大伟人黄帝"，下方标有"中国民族开国之始祖"。

由于《黄帝魂》的深刻影响，在1904年至1905年之间，尊黄思潮十分高涨。当时的一些进步报刊如《江苏》杂志、《国民日日报》等分别刊登黄帝肖像，并公开使用黄帝纪元。尊黄帝为始祖、为国魂的论述层出不穷。1905年，黄节在《国粹学报》上连载《黄史》。同年，许之衡在该刊第6期发表《读〈国粹学报〉感言》。文中说："国魂者，立国之本也。"这些情况表明，船山的民族主义思想，特别是其《黄书》在辛亥革命的前期的确发挥了巨大的启蒙作用。这一时期尊黄帝思潮的兴起，极大地提高了轩辕黄帝在中国历史上的地位，中华民族在黄帝的伟大旗帜引领下，加快了民族融合与团结。

从20世纪40年代初，许多学者对黄帝时代历史人物的资料进行了比较系统的整理。特别是在抗日战争中，中华民族汇聚在黄帝的旗帜下，同仇敌忾，共御外侮，取得了抗日战争的伟大胜利。

in Chinese history, noting that the emperor established the central state, that all vassal states were obedient to and supported him, and that the society maintained a state of peace and harmony for thousands of years. However, after the Qin and Han dynasties, the state went "from extreme unity to disorder, from disorder to separation, and from separation back into unity again." The purpose of *Huangshu* was to rectify errors and return to the ideology of Huangdi, in the hope that the rulers could correct their mistakes through reflection and realize the harmonious society intended by the Yellow Emperor.

The fourth wave occurred when nationalism arose at the end of the Qing Dynasty. *Huangshu* was regarded as the banner of the democratic revolution and an upsurge in honoring Huangdi was ignited. The most important representative figure at that time was Zhang Taiyan, who highly praised the book. In 1901, Zhang Taiyan directly quoted from the important statements in *Huangshu* to publicize his nationalist philosophy. In 1902, in *Book of Qiu*, Zhang wrote, "Reading *Huangshu* indicates that we are all descendants of Huangdi." Zhang played a leading role in promoting *Huangshu* in the late Qing Dynasty. In 1903, Huang Zao edited and published *Soul of Huangdi* with a note saying that the authors were "mostly descendants of the Yellow Emperor" and that the editor was "one of the descendants." The book included 29 articles in its first edition and 44 in its second in 1911. The book was chronicled with the Yellow Emperor Calendar. The title page contained a portrait of Huangdi, with the words "The World's First Great Nationalist HUANGDI" at the top of the portrait and "The Founding Father of the Chinese Nation" underneath.

Due to the profound influence of *Soul of Huangdi*, the wave of honoring the Yellow Emperor remained very high between 1904 and 1905. At that time, certain progressive newspapers, such as *Jiangsu Magazine* and *National Day Daily*, published his portrait and publicly used the Yellow Emperor Calendar. There was continuous discussion about honoring him as the first ancestor and soul of the nation. In 1905, Huang Jie serialized *History of Huangdi* in the *Journal of Chinese Quintessence*. In the same year, Xu Zhiheng published the *Testimonial to Reading the Journal of Chinese Quintessence* in the sixth issue of the journal, which said, "The soul of the country is the foundation of the nation." All these means of acknowledging Huangdi showed that Wang Fuzhi's nationalist

《黄帝魂》
Soul of Huangdi

  中华人民共和国成立，开创了中华民族崭新的时代，也为黄帝文化研究提供了最广泛、最有力的支持。20世纪80年代初，随着中国改革开放，文化事业也得到迅猛发展，学术界开始了黄帝文化研究。特别是20世纪90年代初，旅游业发展迅猛，一些地方政府成立了专业的旅游主管部门，实施"文化搭台，经贸唱戏"，开发旅游，寻根问祖，使得祭拜人文始祖黄帝的热潮更加高涨。

ideals, expressed especially in *Huangshu*, played a key role in the enlightenment in the early stage of the Revolution of 1911. The fourth wave greatly enhanced Huangdi's status in Chinese history and accelerated the integration and unity of the Chinese nation under the great banner of the Yellow Emperor.

From the early 1940s, many scholars systematically sorted the materials concerning historical figures in the Yellow Emperor era. Particularly in the War of Resistance against Japanese Aggression, the Chinese nation gathered under the banner of Huangdi, united against foreign aggression, and secured a great victory.

The founding of the People's Republic of China ushered in a new era for the Chinese nation and provided the most extensive and powerful support for the study of Huangdi culture. In the early 1980s, with China's reform and opening up to the world, the cultural cause also developed rapidly, and, the academic scholars began to study Huangdi's legacy. Especially in the early 1990s, the tourism industry grew quickly. Some local governments established professional tourism departments to carry out the policy of "culture as platform, with economy and trade as leading roles" to develop tourism. These departments searched for the roots and ancestors of Chinese culture, leading to the upsurge of worshiping Huangdi as the first ancestor of Chinese civilization.

乐舞敬拜黄帝
Music and Dance to Worship Huangdi

二、历代祭拜黄帝

1. 五帝、三代时期

黄帝在荆山炼铜铸鼎,鼎成之日与世长辞。他的大臣左彻用木雕刻成黄帝像,取其衣冠几杖设庙祭祀。

颛顼是五帝中的第二帝。他在执政时"令飞龙作效八风之音,命之曰《承云》",以祭祀黄帝。帝喾、帝尧、帝舜执政时祭祀黄帝都是国典,即于明堂祭祀。周代祭祀是把黄帝作为始祖进行祭祀。春秋时期,郑国名相子产兴起了三月三登具茨山祭祀轩辕黄帝活动,并形成祭祀民俗延续至今。

木雕黄帝像
Wooden Statue of the Yellow Emperor

2. 秦、汉时期

秦灵公时,于吴阳祭黄帝。秦献公时,于雍城祭黄帝。秦始皇统一六国后,仍行祭祀黄帝。西汉王朝建立,刘邦称帝。他颁下诏书说:

II. Worship of Huangdi in All Dynasties

1. Five Legendary Rulers and Three Dynasties(c. 2600 BC-221 BC)

The Yellow Emperor smelted copper, cast a cauldron in Jingshan, and died when it was finished. As mentioned above, one of his ministers, Zuoche, carved a wooden statue of the Yellow Emperor and established a temple to make sacrifices to him.

Zhuanxu, the second among the Five Legendary Rulers, "ordered the dragon to make the sound of the winds from eight directions and named the music Chengyun" to make a sacrifice to the Yellow Emperor. During the reign of Emperor Ku, Emperor Yao and Emperor Shun, worship of Huangdi was a national custom, performed in the Ming Hall. In the Zhou Dynasty, Huangdi was offered sacrifices as the first ancestor. During the Spring and Autumn Period, the famous Prime Minister Zichan of the Zheng State initiated the activity of climbing Jucishan Mountain on March 3 to offer sacrifices to the Yellow Emperor, which formed a ritual folklore that continues to this day.

2. Qin and Han Dynasties (221 BC-220 AD)

Emperor Linggong of the Qin Dynasty worshiped Huangdi in Wuyang while Emperor Xiangong worshiped him in Yongcheng. After the First Emperor of Qin united the other six states, he continued to worship Huangdi. When the Western Han Dynasty was established and Liu Bang proclaimed himself emperor, he issued an edict, saying, "I pay great attention to the shrine, and from now on, Huangdi and other gods should be offered sacrifices according to time and customs." Later, Emperor Wen constructed a temple in Weiyang to worship the Five Legendary Rulers. In the winter of 110 BC, the first year of Emperor Wu, he made a trip north to Qiaoshan to offer sacrifices to Huangdi on his way back to Chang'an (now Xi'an), the capital of China at the time. In the Eastern Han Dynasty, Liu Xiu, Emperor Guangwu, established Luoyang as his capital. The worship of Huangdi was still conducted according to the ancient system when the Ming Hall was built.

"吾甚重祠而敬祭。今上帝之祭及山川诸神当祠者，各以其时礼祠之如故。"其后汉文帝又于渭阳作五帝庙行祭五帝。汉武帝于元封元年，即公元前110年冬，去北方巡视还都长安时，专程到桥山祭祀黄帝。东汉，汉光武帝刘秀建都洛阳，其祭祀仍承古制，建筑明堂，祭祀黄帝。

3. 魏、晋、南北朝时期

这一时期，祭祀黄帝主要有三种形式：一是按照汉代惯例祭祀，二是在明堂祭祀，三是到传说有黄帝遗迹的地方祭祀。魏明元帝、魏太武帝和魏文成帝等也在河北涿鹿桥山祭祀黄帝。

4. 隋、唐、宋、元、明、清时期

隋唐时期，仍遵旧制祭祀黄帝。到了唐玄宗李隆基天宝六年，即公元747年，在京城设五帝庙，开启了京城祭祀的先河。宋徽宗时，在京城兴建宝宫，置殿曰神灵，以祠黄帝。元代在大都（今北京）城内建三皇庙，供奉伏羲、神农、黄帝。明清时期仍袭旧制，祭祀黄帝。明太祖朱元璋在洪武四年，即公元1371年祭黄帝文中说，"君生上古，继天立

清世祖顺治像
Portrait of Emperor Shizu Shunzhi of the Qing Dynasty

3. Wei, Jin, Southern and Northern Dynasties (220 AD-581 AD)

During this period, there were three main ways to offer sacrifices to Huangdi. The first was to follow the customs of the Han Dynasty. The second was held in the Ming Hall, and the third was held in the place with the relics of the Yellow Emperor according to the legends. Emperor Mingyuan, Emperor Taiwu and Emperor Wencheng of the Wei Dynasty also offered sacrifices to him at Qiaoshan in Zhuolu, Hebei Province.

4. Sui, Tang, Song, Yuan, Ming, and Qing Dynasties (581 AD-1911 AD)

In the Sui and Tang dynasties, sacrifices continued to be offered to Huangdi. In 747 AD, Li Longji, Emperor Xuanzong of the Tang Dynasty, set up a temple of the Five Legendary Rulers in the capital, where the first sacrificial ceremony was held. During the reign of Emperor Huizong of the Song Dynasty, a treasure palace was built in the capital, named Shenling, to offer sacrifices to Huangdi. In the Yuan Dynasty, Sanhuang Temple was built in Dadu (today's Beijing) to worship Fuxi, Shennong, and Huangdi. In the Ming and Qing dynasties, the old system was still followed to worship Huangdi. In the fourth year of Hongwu, in 1371 AD, Zhu Yuanzhang, Emperor Taizu of the Ming Dynasty, said in his sacrifices to Huangdi, "You were born in ancient times, chosen to be an emperor by heaven, and succeeded in making great achievements, benefiting your descendants." Emperors Daizong, Yingzong, Wuzong, Shizong, and Xizong of the Ming Dynasty, as well as Emperors Shizu Shunzhi to Wenzong Xianfeng of the Qing Dynasty, all offered sacrifices to him. Ritual texts survived for the sacrifices offered during the Ming and Qing dynasties.

5. Worship of Huangdi Since Modern Times

Ritual texts by Sun Yat-sen and Mao Zedong also eulogized the virtues of Huangdi. Sun Yat-sen wrote, "China was founded 5,000 years ago. Huangdi was praised from ancient times for creating the south-pointing cart and pacifying Chiyou chaos. China led world civilization." Similarly, Mao Zedong said, "The famous ancestor founded China, leaving successive descendants. Clever and wise, his light was shining. He built the great cause, standing out in the East."

极，作蒸民主，神功胜德，垂泽于今。"明代宗、英宗、武宗、世宗一直到熹宗均祭祀黄帝，并有祭文存世。清朝时期清世祖顺治到文宗咸丰历代皇帝均祭祀黄帝并有祭文存世。

5. 近代以来祭拜黄帝

孙中山、毛泽东都有祭词祭文，以歌颂轩辕黄帝的功德。如孙中山先生的祭文写道："中华开国五千年，神州轩辕自古传。创造指南车，平定蚩尤乱。世界文明，唯有我先。"如毛泽东祭黄帝词曰："赫赫始祖，吾华肇造；胄衍祀绵，岳峨河浩。聪明睿知，光被遐荒；建此伟业，雄立东方……"

新中国成立后，拜祖祭祖活动更加兴盛。河南省新郑市黄帝故里拜

黄帝故里拜祖大典盛况
Ancestor Worship Ceremony in the Hometown of the Yellow Emperor

寻根拜祖
Ceremony of Seeking Root and Worshiping Ancestor

After the founding of the People's Republic of China, ancestor worship activities prospered. Today, these activities include the Yellow Emperor's hometown worship ceremony in Xinzheng, Henan Province, Qingming Qiaoshan's Yellow Emperor worship in Huangling, Shaanxi Province, the Three Ancestors' Hall sacrificial ceremony in Zhuolu, Hebei Province, and Yellow Emperor Xuanyuan worship in Jinyun, Zhejiang Province and in Huangshan, Anhui Province. These worship activities have been held to high standards; they involve new topics, large scale events, and special characters and are characterized by a strong sense of culture and wide influence. The cosmopolitan nature, popularity, and local characteristics of folk culture improve Huangdi's popularity

祖大典、陕西省黄陵县清明节桥山祭黄帝、河北省涿鹿县"三祖堂"祭祀、浙江省缙云县公祭轩辕黄帝典礼、安徽省黄山市拜轩辕黄帝大典等祭拜活动，规格高、主题新、规模大、亮点多、文化浓、影响广，成为具有世界性、人民性和地方特色的民俗文化。这些祭拜活动在海内外知名度、美誉度不断提升，彰显了黄帝文化的独特魅力。

特别是河南省新郑市每年一度的黄帝故里拜祖大典，共拜始祖，共缅祖德。全球每年都有200余家媒体500余名记者对拜祖大典进行广泛报道，全球110家华语电台联手对大典进行全程直播，真正实现了全球同拜人文始祖轩辕黄帝。它向全世界表明中华儿女维护祖国统一和民族团结的坚强决心和信心，表达了亿万华人同根、同祖、同源，追求和平、和睦、和谐，共享安定、祥和、幸福生活的愿望。

拜祖大典体现了时代性、广泛性、层次性、互动性、仪式性，充分彰显了黄帝文化魅力、炎黄儿女亲和力、民族凝聚力、经济社会推动力。新郑黄帝故里拜祖大典是全球华人的盛大节日，是中华民族融合团结的兴邦盛典，是盛世中华兴旺繁荣的和谐盛典。

and reputation at home and abroad, revealing the unique charm of Huangdi culture.

In particular, the annual ancestor worship ceremony in Xinzheng City of Henan Province attracts people to worship their shared ancestor, Huangdi, together. Every year, more than 500 journalists from more than 200 media outlets around the world cover the ceremony extensively, and 110 Chinese radio stations around the world jointly broadcast the ceremony live. Hence, the first ancestor of humanity is worshiped globally. This event demonstrates to the world the strong determination and confidence of the sons and daughters of the Chinese nation to safeguard the reunification of the motherland and national unity. It expresses the wishes of hundreds of millions of Chinese people to pursue peace, amity, and harmony and to enjoy a stable, peaceful, and happy life with the same root, ancestor, and homology.

The ancestor worship ceremony embodies the traits of modernity, connectedness, hierarchy, interactivity, and ritual. It fully demonstrates the cultural charm of the Yellow Emperor, the affinity of the Yan Emperor and the Yellow Emperors' children, national cohesion, and the driving force of the economy and society. It is also a grand festival for Chinese people all over the world, representing integration, unity and the harmonious prosperity of the Chinese nation.

三、黄帝文化研究

1. 理论研究

　　1991年，中华炎黄文化研究会正式成立。在成立大会上，莅临大会的时任中共中央政治局常委李瑞环同志发表了重要讲话，他指出："中华炎黄文化也可以说就是中华民族文化，博大精深，源远流长，影响深远，是祖先留给我们的一份极其丰厚、极其珍贵的遗产。在当今世界上，凡是炎黄子孙，不管他走到什么地方，只要他良知未泯，都不能不为辉煌灿烂的中华民族文化而感到自豪。"在此感召下，中华炎黄文化研究会在研究和弘扬黄帝文化、开展文化交流等方面做出了突出贡献。随着各省市炎黄文化研究会的先后成立，在中国范围内逐渐形成了研究黄帝文化的热潮。

　　中华炎黄文化研究会编辑的《炎黄汇典》于2002年12月正式出版，产生了广泛的影响，许多著名的学术大家和活跃在全国第一线的学者掀起了研究黄帝文化的热潮。特别是中华炎黄文化研究会创办的《炎黄文化研究》，更是黄帝文化研究的重要刊物。

《炎黄汇典·图像卷》
Collection of Yan Huang

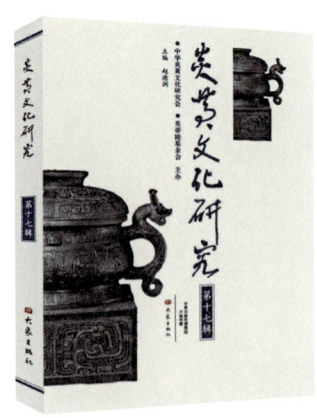

《炎黄文化研究》
Study on Yan Huang Culture

III. Research on Huangdi Culture

1. Theoretical Research

In 1991, the Association for Yan Huang Culture of China was formally established. At the inaugural meeting, Li Ruihuan, a member of the Standing Committee of the Political Bureau of the Communist Party of China (CPC) Central Committee at that time, made an important speech. He pointed out that, "The Yan Huang culture of China can be said to be that of the Chinese nation. It is broad and profound with a long history and far-reaching influence. It is an extremely rich and precious heritage left to us by our ancestors. In today's world, wherever a Chinese descendant goes, as long as he retains his conscience, he cannot but feel proud of the splendid Chinese culture." Following this inspiration, the association has made outstanding contributions to the research and promotion of Huangdi culture and the development of cultural exchanges. With the successive establishment of the Association for Yan Huang Culture in various cities and provinces, a rising trend in studying Huangdi culture has occurred in China.

Collection of Yan Huang, edited by the Association for Yan Huang Culture of China, was published in December 2002. It has exerted a wide influence and promoted the study of Huangdi culture among famous Chinese scholars in related fields. *Study on Yan Huang Culture*, created by the Association for Yan Huang Culture of China, is also an important journal for the study of Huangdi culture.

Since the 1990s, the study of Huangdi culture has flourished throughout the country. Experts and scholars have picked up their pens to write books, and the Associations for Yan Huang Culture and related organizations all over the country have organized academic discussions and published collections of papers. Especially since the beginning of the 21st century, scholarly books on the topic have emerged in an endless stream, including Zhao Guoding's *First Ancestor of Chinese Civilization*, Qu Chen's *Historic Mystery of the Yellow Emperor*, Wang Yi and Sheng Ruiyu's *Complete Book of the Yellow Emperor's Yinfu Classic*, Wang Junyi and Huang Aiping's *Yan Huang Culture and National Spirit*, Chen Guying's *Present Notes and Interpretation of the Yellow Emperor's Four Classics*,

从20世纪90年代开始，黄帝文化研究在全国蓬勃兴起。专家、学者纷纷拿起手中之笔著书立说，全国各地的炎黄文化研究会及相关组织，开展学术讨论，纵论黄帝文化，又将论文结集出版。特别是进入21世纪以来，研究黄帝文化的著作更是层出不穷。如赵国鼎编著《中华文明始祖黄帝》，曲辰著《轩辕黄帝史迹之谜》，王毅、盛瑞裕编著《黄帝阴符经全书》，王俊以、黄爱平编《炎黄文化与民族精神》，陈鼓应著《黄帝四经今注今译》，袁子淦编著《先祖·轩辕黄帝》，张维华主编《黄帝故里——新郑》，何炳武、方光华编著《黄帝的祭典》，何炳武著《黄帝与中华文化》，许顺湛著《五帝时代研究》，刘文学主编《黄帝故里志》，高林华、刘五一主编《文明圣典》，张新斌、刘五一主编《黄帝与中华姓氏》，刘宏民、刘如江著《黄帝文化学》等，从不同侧面反映出黄帝文化是中华文明的肇端和正源。这些研究著作的出版发行，不仅代表了这些年来理论界、学术界的最新研究成果，更重要的是对黄帝文化的一种唤醒，唤醒人们正确看待文明问题、文化问题和信仰问题，并用实际行动来继承和弘扬黄帝文化。

2. 举办研讨会

为弘扬黄帝文化，促进中国社会主义文化繁荣发展，自20世纪以来，全国各省市炎黄文化研究会先后开展了炎黄文化研讨活动。1992年10月，中华炎黄文化研究会、河南省炎黄文化研究会在新郑召开"炎黄文化与中原文明"学术研讨会。1993年，河南炎黄文化研究会与河洛文化研究所在巩义举办"炎黄文化与河洛文明"学术研讨会。1994年在濮阳举办"炎黄文化与龙文化"学术研讨会。1998年10月28日，中国古都学会第15届年会暨新郑古都与中原文明学术研讨会在新郑召开。在此时期，河南、陕西、甘肃、山西、河北、安徽、江西、湖南、湖北、浙江等省市先后举办了黄帝文化研讨活动。

Yuan Zigan's *First Ancestor Xuanyuan*, Zhang Weihua's *The Yellow Emperor's Hometown: Xinzheng*, He Bingwu and Fang Guanghua's *Sacrificial Ceremony of the Yellow Emperor*, He Bingwu's *Yellow Emperor and Chinese Culture*, Xu Shunzhan's *Study on the Age of the Five Legendary Rulers*, Liu Wenxue's *Records of the Yellow Emperor's Hometown*, Gao Linhua and Liu Wuyi's *Canon of Civilization*, Zhang Xinbin and Liu Wuyi's *The Yellow Emperor and Chinese Surnames*, and Liu Hongmin and Liu Rujiang's *Cultural Studies of the Yellow Emperor*, among others. These books consider Huangdi culture as the origin and source of Chinese civilization from various perspectives. They represent the latest academic and theoretical research achievements, and, more importantly, awaken readers to viewing the problems of civilization, culture, and belief correctly and taking practical actions to inherit and promote Huangdi culture.

《黄帝故里志》
Records of the Yellow Emperor's Hometown

《黄帝文化学》
Cultural Studies of the Yellow Emperor

2. Holding Seminars

Since the 20th century, the Associations for Yan Huang Culture of cities and provinces in China have carried out activities to promote Huangdi culture and accelerate the prosperity and development of Chinese socialist culture. In October 1992, the Associations for Yan Huang Culture of China and of Henan held an academic seminar on "Yan Huang culture and Central Plains civilization"

通过研讨，专家、学者一致认为黄帝文化是人类社会特有的一种文化现象，它是中华民族社会实践的结晶，是一种社会精神力量，是中华民族精神的灵魂。黄帝文化的传承与弘扬，促进了中华优秀文化的创新与发展，反映出中华文化具有博大精深而又守正创新的生命力。它对于积极培育和践行社会主义核心价值观，促进民族团结，引领社会进步，都具有深远的历史意义和重大的现实意义。

具茨山与中华文明学术研讨会
Academic Seminar on Jucishan Mountain and Chinese Civilization

3. 黄帝文化国际论坛

进入21世纪以来，中华炎黄文化研究会，各省、市、县炎黄文化研究会相继举办了数百场黄帝文化论坛演讲活动，收到了良好效果。自2007年至今，中华炎黄文化研究会、河南省黄帝故里文化研究会、河南新郑黄帝故里文化研究会已连续14届成功举办了"黄帝文化国际论坛"。论坛对黄帝和黄帝文化进行多角度、多层面、多学科的探讨，把对黄帝的敬仰转化为体认，把远眺转化为近思，把对黄帝文化的弘扬转化为对黄帝子孙的思想教育和道德培育。

in Xinzheng. In 1993, the Association for Yan Huang Culture of Henan and the Heluo Cultural Research Institute co-hosted an academic seminar on "Yan Huang culture and Heluo cvilization" in Gongyi. In 1994, an academic seminar was held on "Yan Huang culture and dragon culture" in Puyang. On October 28, 1998, the 15th annual meeting of the Chinese Ancient Capital Society and the academic seminar on Xinzheng ancient capital and Central Plains civilization was held in Xinzheng. Meanwhile, Henan, Shaanxi, Gansu, Shanxi, Hebei, Anhui, Jiangxi, Hunan, Hubei, Zhejiang and other provinces also organized cultural research activities on Huangdi culture.

Through these seminars, experts and scholars agree that Huangdi culture is a unique phenomenon in human society. It is the crystallization of the social practice of the Chinese nation, a kind of social spiritual strength, and the soul of the Chinese nation's spirit. Its inheritance and promotion have enhanced the innovation and development of Chinese culture, which reflects its broad, profound, upright, and pioneering vitality. It has far-reaching historical and practical significance for cultivating and practicing socialist core values, as well as for encouraging national unity and social progress.

3. International Forum of Huangdi Culture

Since the beginning of the 21st century, the Associations for Yan Huang Culture at different levels have sponsored hundreds of speeches about the Huangdi cultural forum with productive results. Since 2007, the Association for Yan Huang Culture of China, Henan Yellow Emperor's Hometown Cultural Research Association, and Henan Xinzheng Yellow Emperor's Hometown Cultural Research Association have successfully held the International Forum of Huangdi Culture for 14 consecutive sessions. Studies of the Yellow Emperor and his culture have been conducted from multiple angles, levels, and disciplines, allowing admiration of Huangdi to be transformed into recognition, oversight into close consideration, and the promotion of Huangdi culture into the ideological education and moral cultivation of his descendants.

In these forums, well-known experts and scholars from China and abroad talked freely about Huangdi culture and discussed its national construction and development in terms of contemporary China. The seminars involved discussions

历届论坛上，来自国内外的知名专家、学者在畅谈黄帝文化的同时，又根据当代中国实际探讨国家建设与发展，从弘扬黄帝文化，弘扬中华优秀传统文化，讲到中国的政治、经济、军事、科技……影响既深且远。"黄帝文化国际论坛"已经成为一个有高度、有深度、有广度、有温度的论坛，一个有情义、有情操、有情怀的论坛，被誉为"华语第一论坛""中国十大影响力会议""全国最受关注的节庆论坛"。

黄帝文化国际论坛
International Forum of Huangdi Culture

of Huangdi culture and traditional Chinese culture, as well as of politics, economics, military, science, and technology. The effects of these conversations are deep and far-reaching. The International Forum of Huangdi Culture has become a forum with height, depth, and breadth, as well as friendship, sentiment, and feeling. It is known as the "No. 1 forum in the Chinese language," one of "China's top 10 influential conferences," and "the most popular festival forum in China."

炎黄文化节拜祖
Ancestor Worship at the Yan Huang Cultural Festival

四、黄帝文化传播

黄帝文化的传承与弘扬在中国国内已经建立起稳固的组织体系、理论体系和传播体系。而在国外，这些体系虽然还未得以建立，但国内与国外交流体系已经建立。

1. 拜祖大典仪式传播

新郑是轩辕黄帝的出生地、创业地、建都地，祭祀黄帝从五帝时代至今从未间断过。1992年至2005年，新郑连续举办了14届炎黄文化节及公拜始祖轩辕黄帝大典。自2006年升格为省级及国家级主办，至今已举办了15届。经过15年的培育，拜祖大典已经成为一个广为人知的文化品牌，成为全球亿万华人瞩目的拜祖盛典，每年一度的拜祖大典，吸引了世界各国各界嘉宾亲临盛会，拜谒轩辕黄帝。

海外华人寻根拜祖
Overseas Chinese at the Seeking Root and Worshiping Ancestor Festival

IV. Spread of Huangdi Culture

The inheritance and promotion of Huangdi culture have established stable organizational, theoretical and communication systems in China. Though these systems have not yet been implemented in foreign countries, the exchange systems between China and abroad have already been initiated.

1. Spread of the Ancestor Worship Ceremony

Xinzheng is Huangdi's birthplace, where he built a career and a country, and where ancestor worship activities from the Period of the Five Legendary Rulers have never been interrupted. From 1992 to 2005, Xinzheng held 14 consecutive Yan Huang Cultural Festivals and Grand Ceremonies to Worship the First Ancestor. Since 2006, the ancestor worship ceremony has been upgraded to provincial and national levels and has been held for 15 sessions. After 15 years of cultivation, the ancestor worship ceremony has become a well-known cultural brand and an event watched by millions of Chinese around the world. It attracts guests from all walks of life around the world to show respect for Huangdi.

The ancestor worship ceremony at the Yellow Emperor's hometown attracts guests from the Chinese Entrepreneur Association, World Chinese Businessman Association, Chinese Friendship Association, and Chinese Peace Promotion Association. It further draws guests from other organizations, such as Overseas Chinese Chambers of Commerce, Trade and Culture Promotion Associations, Associations of Home Fellows, Research Societies, Federations of Overseas Chinese, and Family Name Associations. These guests come from more than 100 countries and regions, including the United States, Australia, India, Canada, France, Italy, Spain, Austria, Germany, the Netherlands, South Korea, Belgium, Ireland, Hungary, Indonesia, Singapore, the Philippines, Russia, Serbia, Montenegro, Malaysia, Thailand, Japan, and Chinese Hong Kong, Macao, and Taiwan. As an effective means of promoting Huangdi culture, the ancestor worship ceremony at the Yellow Emperor's hometown attracts Chinese people from all over the world to gather in Xinzheng and encourages the study and spread of Huangdi culture throughout the world.

黄帝故里拜祖大典，有来自美国、澳大利亚、印度、加拿大、法国、意大利、西班牙、奥地利、德国、荷兰、韩国、比利时、爱尔兰、匈牙利、印度尼西亚、新加坡、菲律宾、俄罗斯、塞尔维亚、黑山、马来西亚、泰国、日本和中国香港、中国澳门、中国台湾等100多个国家和地区的华人企业家协会、世界华商协会、华人联谊会、中国和平促进会等各类华人华侨商会，贸促会、文化促进会、同乡会、研究会、华侨华人社团联合会等社团组织和姓氏宗亲会嘉宾出席拜祖大典。黄帝故里拜祖大典是弘扬黄帝文化的一种有效载体，它吸引着世界华人在新郑汇集，促进了黄帝文化研究和黄帝文化在世界上的传播。

炎黄二帝塑像
Statues of the Yan and Huang Emperors

　　为进一步传承弘扬黄帝文化，促进黄帝文化在海外的传播，凝聚全世界炎黄子孙共筑中华民族伟大复兴梦的精神力量，河南新郑黄帝故里文化研究会联合河南省黄帝故里基金会、河南根文创文化产业有限公司等单位，精工制作了重达60余吨的炎黄二帝塑像，捐赠美国休斯敦黄氏

百家姓拜祖团
Ancestor Worship Group of Hundred Family Surnames

To promote the spread of Huangdi culture, Xinzheng Yellow Emperor's Hometown Cultural Institute, Henan Yellow Emperor's Hometown Foundation, Henan Root Culture Co. Ltd. and other units produced two statues of the Yan and Yellow Emperors, weighing more than 60 tons. They donated them to the Huang Clan Association of Houston, United States. Hence, the statues are worshiped by overseas Chinese for the first time. Every year on the third day of the third month of the lunar calendar, overseas Chinese in the United States hold a ceremony to worship Huangdi at the same time as the ancestor worship ceremony in the Yellow Emperor's hometown.

Yan Huang culture is the source of the deepest historical memory for Chinese people all over the world. The value of the concept of the "unity of man and nature, harmony in diversity" has been recognized by most of Chinese people, representing affinity for Chinese people at home and abroad. The ancestor worship held in the hometown of the Yellow Emperor has a wide influence. The annual ancestor worship ceremony is broadcast live by the CCTV Entertainment Channel, International Channel, and Hong Kong Satellite TV. More than 100

宗亲会,炎黄二帝塑像首次在海外供炎黄子孙瞻仰。每年农历三月三,美国华人华侨将同期举办恭拜黄帝典礼,实现与黄帝故里拜祖大典同步祭拜轩辕黄帝。

炎黄文化是全球华人历史记忆最深的源头。黄帝文化具有的"天人合一、和而不同"的价值理念,在国内外得到了广大华人的认可,这是炎黄子孙在海内外很重要的一个认同标志。黄帝故里拜祖大典层次高、规模大、影响广,每年的拜祖大典都由央视文艺频道、国际频道、香港卫视全程直播。国内外有百余家新闻媒体报道大典盛况。在长达四个半小时的联播中,主创人员特别策划了"此时此刻全球瞩目"环节,实现了多国家、多语种、多媒体国际大联播,在海内外引起强烈反响。多年来,郑州电视台携手海内外50家华语电视台进行拜祖大典国际大联播,并以46种语言向全世界进行转播。近年来,拜祖活动中还增加了微博、微信、手机APP等传播方式,并通过图文弹窗、上传视频、话题设置的形式,对拜祖大典进行全方位、多角度、多层次的宣传报道,将拜祖大典盛况传播至世界各地。

2.《黄帝内经》在国外

《黄帝内经》不仅是一部医学典籍,而且是一部"治国之本"的经典。它为海内外炎黄子孙重新认识黄帝,弘扬黄帝文化提供了可靠的史料依据。

在"一带一路"倡议以及中国文化"走出去"背景下,《黄帝内经》英文译本在海外发行,形成了一种特有范式,可谓"中西交融、优势互补,系统推进,层层深入"。《黄帝内经》所蕴含的丰富的中医文化内涵被传译出来,成为中国文化海外传播过程中进一步"走出去"的一条探索路径。

《黄帝内经》是黄帝文化的重要组成部分,它的主要内容是中医药的兴起和中医药理论的建立。它是中国中医药文化的根和源。《黄帝内

news media at home and abroad report the grand ceremony. In the four and a half hours of network broadcast, the website link "Global Attention at This Moment," created particularly for the event, reveals the multiple countries, languages, and media outlets involved in broadcasting the event internationally. For many years, the Zhengzhou TV Station, in collaboration with 50 Chinese TV stations at home and abroad, has internationally broadcast the ancestor worship ceremony in 46 languages. In recent years, modern media, such as microblog, WeChat, and mobile APP, have been employed. With graphic pop-up windows, uploaded videos, and topic settings, the ancestor worship ceremony is reported in an all-round, multi-angle, and multi-level way, and the grand ceremony is spread around the world.

中外媒体联合直播
Chinese and Foreign Media Jointly Broadcast Live

2. Spread of *Huangdi's Internal Classic* Abroad

Huangdi's Internal Classic is not only a canonical medical text but also a classic on "the foundation of governing a country." It provides a reliable historical basis for Chinese descendants at home and abroad to reacquaint themselves with Huangdi and promote Huangdi culture.

经》在海外的传播，主要是通过英文翻译得以实现的。到目前为止，国内外《黄帝内经》英译本近20种。进入21世纪以来，《黄帝内经》在海外的传播呈现出繁荣发展的态势。自2010年中医针灸成功入选世界级非物质文化遗产名录以来，中医日益受到国际社会的广泛关注，并以中国传统医学的重要组成部分加入国际医药卫生合作。截至目前，中医药已在183个国家和地区广泛传播。我国已与外国政府、国际组织签署了86个专门的中医药合作协议，已建立海外中医药中心17个，2018年新增中医药中心等57个中医药国际合作专项项目。

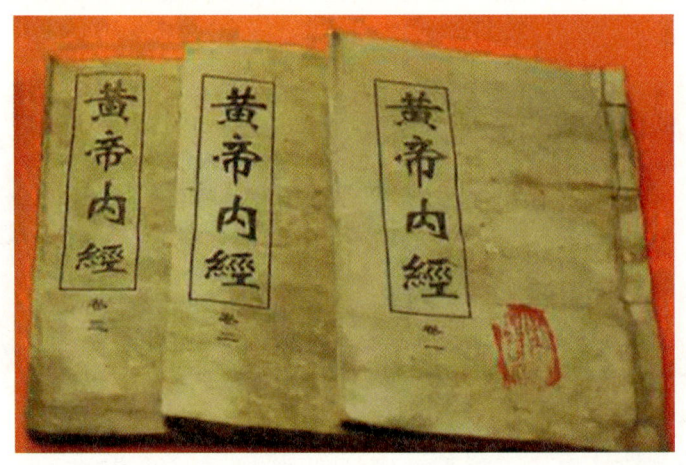

《黄帝内经》
Huangdi's Internal Classic

中医的合法化地位得到越来越多国家和组织的承认：澳大利亚维多利亚州有关中医合法地位的立法得到全国卫生厅长会议的认同，并作为蓝本得以向其他州推广；针灸获得美国食品药品监督管理局（FDA）批准，正式被批准为治疗方法；目前，英国政府正在酝酿对中医药立法。"中医合法化"地位在不同国家和地区的确立，标志着中医药文化在该地区拥有广泛传播的基础。此外孔子学院和国外高校纷纷开设中医课程，如英国在国立大学开设中医和针灸学士学位课程，在教学体制、课

Under the Belt and Road Initiative and in the context of Chinese culture "going out," the English version of *Huangdi's Internal Classic* was published overseas. It has the particular paradigm of the integration of Chinese and Western cultures, complementary advantages, systematic advancement, and deeper layers. Through translation, the rich cultural connotations of traditional Chinese medicine contained in the text have become a path to exploring the process of further spreading Chinese culture overseas.

Huangdi's Internal Classic is a key part of Huangdi culture and the root and source of Chinese medical culture. It mainly presents the emergence of traditional Chinese medicine (TCM) and the establishment of TCM theory. Its overseas spread is principally realized through English translations. So far, there have been nearly 20 English versions of translation at home and abroad. Since the beginning of the 21st century, the text's overseas transmission has prospered. Since acupuncture was successfully included in the World Intangible Cultural Heritage List in 2010, TCM has received increasing attention from the international community and been included in international medical and health activities as an important part of traditional medicine. TCM has now spread to 183 countries and regions, and 86 special traditional Chinese medicine cooperation agreements have been signed with foreign governments and international organizations. Moreover, 17 TCM centers have been established overseas. In 2018, there were 57 new special projects for TCM international cooperation, including TCM centers.

TCM has been legalized in a growing number of countries and organizations. The legislation of TCM in Victoria State of Australia was approved by the National Conference of Health Directors and has been promoted to other states as a model. Acupuncture has also been approved by the United States Food and Drug Administration (FDA) and is officially recognized as a medical treatment. At present, the government of the United Kingdom (UK) is considering legislation on TCM. The legalization of TCM in different countries and regions indicates that TCM culture has a wide basis for its spread in these areas. An ensuing institutional pattern is that various Confucius Institutes or foreign universities are also offering TCM courses. For example, the UK offers bachelor's degree courses in TCM and acupuncture at national universities. Its teaching system, curriculum setting, and selection of high-level Chinese and foreign

程设置、高水平中外教师选配等方面均相当正规。《黄帝内经》作为中医课程的主要教材，相关译介工作也取得了进展，逐步形成了翻译类型多样化、中医术语标准化的趋势。

teachers are appropriately formal. As *Huangdi's Internal Classic* is the main textbook for TCM courses, numerous, diverse translations have been produced and TCM terms have been standardized, both of which help to disseminate awareness of the text abroad.

第四章

黄帝精神弘扬

Chapter 4

Promotion of Huangdi Spirit

黄帝文化犹如中华民族共同体内的血液，已流淌了五千多年，推动了中华文明不断向前发展。在中国历史长河中，黄帝文化以坚韧的生命力和"海纳百川，有容乃大"的气概，在"兼容并蓄"中逐步壮大和丰富起来。

黄帝文化生生不息，黄帝精神历久弥新。黄帝文化精神，是中华民族精神的源头活水。关于黄帝精神，专家学者有着多样的认识和表述。黄帝故里拜祖大典组委会多次组织专家、学者论证，提出了黄帝精神表述语，概括为"鼎新、大公、中和"。黄帝文化精神的具体内涵可在上述6个字的基础上扩展为六种精神：自强不息的奋斗精神、革故鼎新的创造精神、厚德载物的仁德精神、天下为公的正大精神、以人为本的人文精神、中和大同的和谐精神。它对于推进新时代中国特色社会主义建设，实现中华民族伟大复兴，具有重要的指导和借鉴意义。

一、自强不息的奋斗精神

"自强不息"是一种精神，一种美好的品德，是对美好未来的无限憧憬和不懈追求，也是脚踏实地，百折不挠，排除万难，开拓奋进的雄浑气魄。"自强不息"出自《易传》乾卦象辞"天行健，君子以自强不息"，意思是日月星辰刚强劲健不停运行，君子处世应效法天地，刚毅坚卓，发愤图强，与时俱进。乾卦的六句爻辞以潜龙、见龙、惕龙、跃龙、飞龙、亢龙，六条不同的龙作为喻义人自强不息的六个阶段，展现了龙的精神。龙是黄帝时代最伟大的精神文化象征，其特质代表和展示了黄帝文化精神标识与精髓。

黄帝文化之所以产生，一是在一定的历史发展过程中，人们创造了各式各样的物质文化，而且在生产劳动中结成了关系，即生产关系。这种生产关系汇总起来，就形成了社会关系，构成了社会，也诞生了文化。黄帝文化的产生，二是基于物质文化和非物质文化的发展，三是诸

Huangdi culture is like the blood circulating within the Chinese nation and has continuously promoted the development of Chinese civilization for more than 5,000 years. Over China's long history, Huangdi culture has gradually been strengthened, blossoming through its tenacious vitality and spirit of inclusiveness.

Huangdi culture is everlasting, and Huangdi spirit is unfading. Experts and scholars understand Huangdi spirit in various ways. The Organizing Committee of the Yellow Emperor Worship Ceremony has frequently engaged experts to identify the core and essence of Huangdi spirit. As a result, the experts have summarized it with keywords such as innovation, equality, and great unity. These words can be interpreted in relation to the following six spirits, or defining ideologies: the spirit of endless self-improvement, the spirit of innovation, the spirit of clemency, the spirit of equality, the people-oriented spirit, and the spirit of great unity. Huangdi spirit plays an essential role both in guiding and illuminating the construction of socialism with Chinese characteristics in the new era and implementing the Chinese nation's great rejuvenation.

Ⅰ. Spirit of Endless Self-Improvement

"Endless self-improvement" is a spirit, a virtue, infinite wish, and endless pursuit for a better future, which is pragmatic, persevering, and pioneering. "Self-improvement" was referred to in the hexagrams in *Book of Changes* (an ancient philosophical and ethical work), "As Heaven maintains vigor through movement, a gentleman should constantly strive for self-perfection." In other words, just as the sun, the moon, and stars remain strong and robust in their ceaseless motion, so humans should follow the example of heaven, remaining resolute, firm, and persistent to keep up with the times. The six-sentence statements of the hexagrams are metaphors about the six stages of self-improvement with six kinds of dragons—Submerged Dragon, Present Dragon, Watchful Dragon, Leaping Dragon, Flying Dragon, and Hyper Dragon. The dragon is a mighty symbol of the Yellow Emperor era, both spiritually and culturally, and its features represent and reveal the spiritual identity and essence of Huangdi culture.

Huangdi culture was born out of five contexts. First, as people created all kinds of material cultures, relationships were formed in production activities,

文化因子的融合，四是继承和创新文化，五是道德文化。黄帝文化的产生与道德实践有着密不可分的关系，而黄帝文化的产生发展，是通过千百万人顽强的奋斗来改造自然、改造社会、改造人类实现的。从黄帝修德振兵建国，到关乎民生的诸多发明，从以德依法治国，到社会秩序的安定，等等，无一不是黄帝文化自强不息精神的例证。

红山文化·玉龙
Hongshan Culture · Jade Dragon

源于黄帝时期、代代相传的自强不息奋斗精神，是中华民族克服一切艰难险阻，在挫折和困境中奋起，雄踞世界民族之林的不竭动力。自强不息精神，在中国历史上得到了继承和弘扬。人们对自强有着充分的认识和理解，如"自强是脚踏实地，百折不挠，一步一个脚印地向着崇高的理想迈进""自强是对困难的蔑视，对挫折的回应，对成功的向往和渴望"。这都是人民在实践中的总结。唐代李咸用《送人》诗诵道："眼前多少难甘事，自古男儿当自强。"这首诗表达了我们不能苟且偷安，一定要自强不息，才能创出一番事业。自强是中华民族的传统美德，自强是支持着中国人自立于世界民族之林的一种精神，一种信念，一种境界，是流淌在中华民族文明血管中的生生不息的血液，是中国人民代代相传的传世之宝。孔子说："笃行信道，自强不息。" 明代吕

which formed relations of production. These relations of production evolved into social relations, which further became society. Culture was thus created. The second context was based on the development of both material and non-material culture. The third was the integration of various cultural factors. The fourth was the culture of inheritance and innovation. And the last was the moral culture. The emergence of Huangdi culture was closely related to moral practice, and Huangdi culture was achieved through the struggle of millions of people as nature, society, and humanity transformed. Huangdi's cultivation of morals, establishment of the capital, unification of the society, and construction of social order were proofs of the spirit of unremitting self-improvement.

This spirit, which originates from the Yellow Emperor era, has been passed down from generation to generation. It remains an inexhaustible driving force for the Chinese nation to overcome obstacles, rise from countless setbacks, and become one of the most powerful countries in the world. Chinese people have a full understanding of self-improvement, including notions such as "self-

黄帝口碑记
Tablet Inscription at Huangdi Pathway

黄帝口石碑
A Stele at Huangdi Pathway

坤《呻吟语·谈道》:"下手处是自强不息,成就处是至诚无息。"康有为说:"自强为天下健,志刚为大君之道。"在中国历史上,正是有了自强不息的奋斗精神,才有伟大的中华民族继往开来的壮举,才有中华文明发展的锦绣前程。在新时代加快实现中国梦的伟大征程中,中华民族伟大的创造精神、伟大的奋斗精神、伟大的团结精神、伟大的梦想精神等精神品质,与黄帝文化自强不息的奋斗精神合频共振,表现出强大的生命力。

improvement is to keep one's feet on the ground, and to move towards a noble ideal" and "self-improvement is to be fearless in the face of difficulties and to look forward to success." All Chinese people embody these notions in practice. In the Tang Dynasty, Li Xianyong wrote a poem, *See Off*, stating "With plenty of difficulties in front of us, a true man should possess the spirit of self-improvement." This poem indicates that people should not be satisfied with temporary peace, but should seek improvement to make achievements. Self-improvement is the traditional virtue of the Chinese nation. It is a spirit, a belief, and a state that supports the Chinese people in standing out in the world. As Confucius said, "Believe in the right way, and never stop self-improvement." Lü Kun of the Ming Dynasty wrote in his philosophical works *Moaning: on Tao*, "Achievement begins with endless self-improvement and ceaselessly expands with complete sincerity." Kang Youwei said, "Only by self-improvement can the world be improved, and only by perseverance can one become a true man." With the spirit of self-improvement, the great Chinese nation can, therefore, progress into a bright future. In the new era, as the great journey towards the Chinese dream accelerates, the Chinese national spirit of innovation, spirit of fighting, spirit of great unity, and spirit of aspiring resonate with Huangdi's spirit of self-improvement and reveal strong vitality.

二、革故鼎新的创造精神

　　《周易·杂卦》说："革，去故也，鼎，取新也。"这句话意思是去掉旧的，建立新的。越是在社会大变革时期，许多事情越需要革故鼎新。轩辕黄帝是一个富有创新精神的人，其主要体现就是勇于打破旧的体制和制度，创建中国古代国家。黄帝时代有许多发明创造，如"垂衣裳而天下治""黄帝作宝鼎三，以象天地人""黄帝时造书契""黄帝作宫室，以避寒暑"，等等。正是轩辕黄帝为代表的一代伟大先贤不断创新创造，才使得华夏文明出现在中国大地上，处处闪耀着璀璨的光芒。中华文明五千多年起源、形成、壮大的历史，就是一部不断创新的发展史，黄帝的一生，是革故鼎新的一生。

　　中华民族经过五千多年风雨磨砺，早已将革故鼎新精神深深融入人民的血液之中。从创造物质财富到创造精神文化，中华民族的不断成长，中华文明的逐步进步，都彰显了黄帝革故鼎新精神无比强大的创造力、推动力、生命力，深刻影响和改变着我们这个世界。以孔子为代表人物的儒家文化总结、传承并发展了黄帝文化，并逐步成为中华优秀传统文化中的主流文化。孔子开创了变革、变易、创新的哲学，使得中华文化得到大发展、大繁荣。

　　在中国历史上，黄帝文化革故鼎新的创造精神不断得到弘扬。如中国文字的发明，让中华文明五千多年的历史传承不断，历久弥新；古老的中华造纸术、印刷术、火药、指南针四大发明，开启了古代人类文明发展史的新纪元。东汉张衡制造的浑天仪，南北朝时期祖冲之计算出的圆周率，元朝郭守敬的《授时历》，明朝李时珍所著《本草纲目》等一系列伟大创造与发明，无一不是献给人类文明的智慧结晶和创新成果。

Ⅱ. Spirit of Innovation

In *Book of Changes*, it is written, "Reform, to remove the old; innovation, to accept the new." Reforms and innovations are especially needed in major social changes. As an innovator, Xuanyuan Huangdi had the courage to break the old system and establish the ancient Chinese state. Many inventions appeared during the Yellow Emperor era, such as "creating the clothing system 'Chuishang' to govern the country," "casting three cauldrons to represent heaven and earth," "creating characters," and "building palaces to shelter from coldness and heat." Constant innovation by a generation of outstanding talents created a shining Chinese civilization in the Yellow Emperor era. The 5,000-year history of the beginning, formation, and development of Chinese civilization is one of continuous novelty. Huangdi's life was marked by revolution and originality.

After more than 5,000 years of refinement, the spirit of innovation has been deeply rooted in the blood of the Chinese nation. From the increase of wealth to the development of creative spirit, each progressive step of the Chinese nation and civilization demonstrates the incomparably powerful spirit of innovation that has profoundly affected and changed our world. Confucianism, represented by Confucius, has epitomized, drawn on, and evolved Huangdi culture, gradually becoming the core of an outstanding traditional Chinese culture. Confucius pioneered the philosophy of reform, change, and innovation, which enabled Chinese culture to develop and prosper.

The invention of Chinese characters forms part of 5,000-year Chinese civilization. The four great inventions in ancient China—papermaking, gunpowder, printing, and the compass—initiated a new era of ancient human civilization. A series of great creations, including the Armillary Sphere by Zhang Heng in the Eastern Han Dynasty, the Pi (ratio of the circumference of a circle to its diameter) by Zu Chongzhi in the Southern and Northern Dynasties, the *Shoushi Calendar* by Guo Shoujing in the Yuan Dynasty, and the *Compendium of Materia Medica* by Li Shizhen in the Ming Dynasty, are Chinese gems of life and wisdom and have contributed to the development of human civilization.

孔子像
Portrait of Confucius

在当代，中国共产党发扬革故鼎新精神，团结带领全国人民，改革开放，实现了从高度集中的计划经济体制向社会主义市场经济体制的根本性转变，实现了人民生活从温饱向全面小康的转变，综合国力大幅提升。这些成就的取得，主要来源于革故鼎新的创造精神。

《本草纲目》
Compendium of Materia Medica

In the modern era, the Communist Party of China has carried forward the spirit of innovation, uniting and leading the people throughout the country to carry out reform and opening up policy. It has achieved China's fundamental transformation from a centrally planned economy to a vibrant socialist market economy, and transformation from subsistence to an affluent society in all aspects. Comprehensive national power has been greatly increased. These achievements are largely the result of the spirit of innovation.

三、厚德载物的仁德精神

黄帝文化的精髓是道德，是天人合一，是以德化济世。德的根本是"和"，是"生"。"和"是重整体、持公心，"生"是怀利他之心，这就是德。道德，是黄帝文化开出的精神之花，而这精神之花，又深深扎根于人民的生活土壤之中，扎根于中华儿女的心中。轩辕黄帝尊天悟道，通过对人类生命的感悟，把道德实践作为安国兴邦，创建和谐社会，造福天下人民唯此为大的核心价值，可谓人类历史上道德实践的一场革命。这种道德精神在人的思想培育、道德思想光大等方面，都起着十分重要的促进作用。

仁德，最早语出先秦典籍《逸周书·大聚》："生无乏用，死无传尸，此谓仁德。"意为致利除害、爱人无私的大公崇高道德。可见，古人衡量仁德的标准主要为公正与偏私的力行程度，"大公"是最高的崇德境界，崇尚仁德是厚德载物的重要体现。"大公"的准则就是对天地的效法，天人合一实为天地与人有共同的运动变化规律。天无私覆，地无私载，日月无私照，不偏不倚任何人。

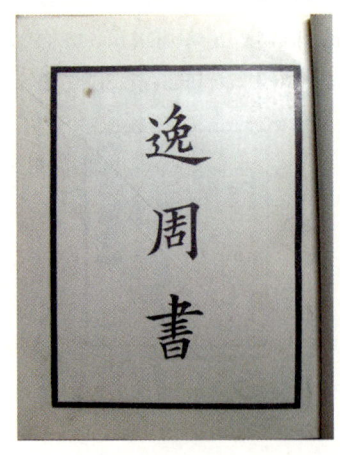

《逸周书》
The Book of the Zhou Dynasty

III. Spirit of Clemency

The essence of Huangdi culture lies in morality, the integrity of man and nature, and blessings granted to the world with moral cultivation. The roots of morality are congruence and altruism; congruence stresses wholeness or justice, while altruism signifies a proclivity to bless others. Morality, the spiritual bloom of Huangdi culture, is deeply rooted in the soil of livelihood for mankind and entrenched in the minds of Chinese nationals. Huangdi respected heaven and attained enlightenment. Through his perception of human life, he regarded moral practice as the core value for the peace and prosperity of his country, a harmonious society, and the benefit of the people. His approach marks a revolution in moral practice in human history, and this moral spirit has a pivotal effect on cultivating man's ideology and morals.

The word "clemency" originated from *The Book of the Zhou Dynasty*, "Clemency is known as living a meaningful life before demise." The term denotes selflessness, justice, and high morality. Hence, the criteria of clemency for ancient man lay in the extent to which he was just and impartial. "Great justice" is the sublime realm of endorsing morality, and the reverence for benevolence is an important embodiment of virtue. The criterion of "great justice" is modelled in the universe, as the integrity of man and nature is, in actuality, a shared rule of movement for both man and the cosmos. Both heaven and earth are not intentionally selfless, and sunlight and moonlight are impartially cast on every individual. Thus, everything in heaven and earth is equal and just.

Historical sources archive some strategies of morality-based country state governance performed during the Yellow Emperor era. For example, *Book of Changes* states, "You can observe the rules of astronomy when looking up and have an eye on geography when looking down, and whereupon you can ascertain the truthfulness of darkness and light." This is a statement about self-cultivation of morality. *Records of the Grand Historian* observes that "Xuanyuan invigorated the army with moral cultivation" and that "he is known as the Yellow Emperor due to his cultivation of morality." *Mister Lü's Spring and Autumn Annals*, in turn, notes that, "There is no better way to govern the world and the state than to use virtue

《周易·系辞上》："仰以观于天文，俯以察于地理，是故知幽明之故。"这句话就是对进德修业的表述。《史记·五帝本纪》："轩辕乃修德振兵""有土德之瑞，故号黄帝"。《吕氏春秋·上德》："为天下及国，莫如以德，莫如行义。以德以义，不赏而民劝，不罚而邪止。此神农、黄帝之政也。"晋王嘉《拾遗记·轩辕黄帝》记述了黄帝时代推行的以德治国："使九行之士以统万国。"这些史料皆记述了黄帝时代推行的以德治国方略。黄帝仁爱百姓，以仁德化民，赢得了民众的拥戴。他通过"修德振兵"，做到协和万邦；通过宽厚仁和，达到海纳百川。他克己奉公，提出"六禁重"：声禁重、色禁重、衣禁重、香禁重、味禁重、室禁重。要求官员节简朴素，反对奢靡并率先垂范，处处带头，严于律己，讲修行、树公义、立公德。黄帝还制定法则法规，规范人们的行为，建立起社会新秩序。

五千多年来，中华历代圣哲先贤，无一不对天下苍生怀有仁爱慈悲之心。颛顼帝绝地通天以制定礼义，理顺四时五行之气以教化万民。帝高辛仁德而威严，温和而守信，修养自身，天下归服。帝尧尊敬有善德的人，使同族九代相亲相爱，各诸侯方国都能和睦相处。帝舜理顺父义、母慈、兄友、弟恭、子孝这五种伦理道德，人民都遵从不违。成汤是商朝的开国始祖，也是一位仁德君王，他不仅爱护百姓，甚至对飞鸟走兽都怀有关爱之心。

中华民族十分注重德行修养。西周著名的政治家周公贤能多才，全心全意辅佐成王，制礼作乐，使国家成为礼仪之邦，为历代圣贤所推崇，给后人留下"周公吐哺，天下归心"的千古佳话。孔子提倡"仁爱"，孟子"富贵不能淫，贫贱不能移，威武不能屈"的品格名言，至今仍是人生德行的准则。荀子主张"仁义"和"以德服人"，彰显出中华民族厚德载物的仁德精神。

and to practice righteousness. With virtue and righteousness, people will strive for good without reward, and evil will be stopped without punishment. This is the rule of Shennong and the Yellow Emperor." *Records of Shiyi* by Wang Jia of the Jin Dynasty provides an account of morality deployed to rule the country in the reign of the Yellow Emperor, who maintained "governance of the entire country by practicing 'Nine Virtues'." With benevolence and virtue toward his people, the Yellow Emperor won the nation's support. He achieved harmony by "invigoration of army force with the cultivation of morality," attaining inclusiveness through generosity and benevolence. Being self-denying and public-spirited, Huangdi proposed the following "six prohibitions": prohibition from lust when appreciating music, prohibition from obsession with women, prohibition from being overtly demanding regarding garments, prohibition from intensive fragrance, prohibition from overt lush aliment, and prohibition from extravagance in palace decoration. He demanded that his officials practice a simple and thrifty life and oppose extravagance, while he himself led the way in "performing cultivation and being both upright and virtuous." The Yellow Emperor also enacted rules to normalize behavior among the people and entrench new social norms.

For more than 5,000 years, sages of all generations have shown benevolence to and companion for the common people. Emperor Zhuanxu created rites in which people had their own duties and did not interfere with each other. He further rationalized the Solar Terms of the four seasons and Five Elements to enlighten his subjects. Being moderate and honest himself, Emperor Ku (Gaoxin) was keen to promote self-cultivation and thus subordinated the world. Emperor Yao highly revered people with integrity, allowing all generations in the same clan to bond well and all kingdoms to live in harmony. Emperor Shun clarified the five ethics, that is, father's righteousness, mother's kindness, elder brother's friendliness, younger brother's respect, and son's filial piety, so that his people would abide by them and refrain from any breach. Cheng Tang, the first emperor of the Shang Dynasty, was also an emperor of virtue, and showed concerns for his people, maintaining sympathy for all living creatures on earth as well.

The Chinese nation has always highly valued virtues and self-cultivation. The virtuous and versatile Chou Kung, a noted politician in the Western Zhou Dynasty, assisted King Cheng to his utmost of his capacity in ruling the country

帝尧像
Portrait of Emperor Yao

　　仁德精神是中华民族精神的核心，也是英雄模范身上最显著的标识。仁德精神体现在行为上就是爱国、爱民、报国志、报民情。有这样一群人，他们是"最美奋斗者"、"共和国勋章"和国家荣誉称号获得者，他们用感人事迹书写了忠诚报国的不朽诗篇。如钱学森、邓稼先、郭永怀等"两弹一星"元勋，为了锻造大国重器甘愿隐姓埋名；黄大年、李保国、南仁东、钟扬等新时代科学家，创造了辉煌的科技成果；"人民楷模"王继才以海岛为家，坚守32年直至生命结束。又如于漪从教68年不离讲台，于敏"愿将一生献宏谋"；袁隆平90高龄依然在水稻领域攻关不止……他们是实干爱国的模范，是以身报国的英雄，更是"最美道德"践行者。

　　在习总书记培育和践行社会主义核心价值观思想指引下，全国把核心价值观建设贯穿国民教育全过程。如从学校抓起，融入教育教学、校风学风；融入精神文明建设，运用先进典型宣传；建立和规范礼仪制

by launching rites and ceremonies, allowing the kingdom to grow into etiquette and enjoy reverence of sages of all generations. The well-known praise that "the whole world would show their sincere subordination with talents like Chou Kung assisting in governing the country" thus found fame among descendants. Benevolence, advocated by Confucius, and Mencius' motto, "neither riches nor honors can corrupt him; neither poverty nor humbleness can make him swerve from principle; neither threats nor forces can subdue him," remain principles of virtue in life. Xuncius, a famous thinker in late Warring States Period, endorsed "benevolence and righteousness" and "convincing people with virtue," reflecting the spirit of clemency of the Chinese nation.

The spirit of clemency is, therefore, at the core of the Chinese nation and is the most prominent symbol of heroes and models, embodied in behaviors such as patriotism, care for the people, dedication to the nation, and repayment of people's devotion. Various models, such as "the most glamorous fighters," laureates of the Medal of the Republic and state honors record perpetual chapters of loyalty to the country with tear-inducing stories. Pioneers of "atomic and hydrogen bombs and man-made satellites," such as Qian Xuesen, Deng Jiaxian, and Guo Yonghuai, as well as more recent scientists, such as Huang Danian, Li Baoguo, Nan Rendong, and Zhong Yang, continue this tradition. Yuan Longping, the father of hybrid rice, is still working on rice breeding at the age of 90. These figures are all heroes and performers of the "most charming morality."

Guided by President Xi Jinping's cultivation and practice of socialist core values, the nation has woven the core values discussed above into the entire process of national education. In schools, these values are integrated into regular education and teaching, and the construction of school ethos and the spirit of learning. They are used to construct spiritual civilization by cultivating the typical models. In the establishment and normalization of etiquette, they are reflected in all aspects of building civilized cities, villages, and towns, as well as units, households, and campuses. In subliminally promoting people's moral accomplishments and identities, the core values penetrate all phases of the creation, production, and dissemination of spiritual and cultural products. Moral spirit exhibits strong cohesion, which is crucial to the pursuit of value and spiritual affiliation. That the Chinese nation has thrived and developed despite ebbs and

南崖轩辕宫石碑
A Stele in South-cliff Xuanyuan Palace

度,体现到文明城市、文明村镇、文明单位、文明家庭、文明校园创建活动各个方面;融入精神文化产品创作、生产、传播各个环节,潜移默化地增进人们的道德智慧和认同。道德精神具有巨大的凝聚力,这种凝聚力有着深厚的价值追求和精神归属。中华民族在历史沉浮跌宕中之所以生生不息、不断发展,在于它始终承续着博大精深的黄帝文化,承续着厚德载物的仁德精神。

flows in its long history is the result of its inheritance of the vast, magnificent culture of the Yellow Emperor and the spirit of benevolence and virtue.

南崖轩辕宫
South-cliff Xuanyuan Palace

四、天下为公的正大精神

五千多年前,黄帝没有崛起时,"诸侯相侵伐,暴虐百姓",社会秩序混乱,社会物资匮乏,民不聊生。于是黄帝挺身而出,与炎帝战于阪泉,与蚩尤战于涿鹿,逐荤粥于北漠,合兵符于釜山,舍身为民,统一天下,安邦兴国,可谓是天下为公。他坚持崇尚贤能,任人唯贤,胸怀宽广,兼济天下。《管子·地数》记述黄帝问于伯高"吾欲陶天下而以为一家",就是要构建"中华民族共同体"。黄帝天下为公的精神对改善国家间关系,促进合作有重要的启发意义。

古代的圣贤,无一不是把"天下为公"看作衡量执政好坏的标准。如夏禹为了让普天下的黎民百姓早日摆脱洪涝水害之苦,过上安居乐业的稳定生活,每天起早贪黑奋战在劈山填沟、开凿水道、疏浚河流的治水工地,留下数千年口口相传的"三过家门而不入"的佳话。郑相子产

大禹治水
Emperor Yu Taming the Flood

IV. Spirit of Equality

Prior to the rise of the Yellow Emperor, vassals trespassed upon other territories and were tyrannical toward people, and the masses could hardly survive due to the chaotic social order and scarcity of social materials. Therefore, the Yellow Emperor stepped forward and fought with Emperor Yan in Banquan and Chiyou in Zhuolu. By driving Xunyu to the northern section of the desert and holding a Hefu ceremony (a long-established system of alliance tokens in China) at Fushan, Huangdi sacrificed himself for the people and soon declared victory in unifying the country and establishing his kingdom. His example demonstrates that the whole world is for all people. Huangdi believed in showing respect to able and virtuous persons, recruiting people based on their virtue, maintaining an open mind, and considering the world as a whole. According to the book *Guanzi* (a compilation of the statements of various schools of thought from the pre-Qin period), the Yellow Emperor told Bogao, "I am determined to bond the world." That is, he aimed to construct a community with a common fate for the Chinese nation. Huangdi's spirit of the whole world for all people serves as an inspiration for improving relations between countries and promoting cooperation.

Ancient sages deemed "the whole world for all people" to be a criterion to gauge governance. For instance, to help the masses surmount the torments of floods and live happy, stable lives, Xia Yu, the founding king of the Xia Dynasty, spent days and nights at the water control site; he was widely praised for turning away from entering his home three times and instead focusing on finding solutions to the people's problems. Zheng kingdom's Prime Minister Zi Chan refused to claim civilian abodes or farmland as his own. These stories showed that they all regarded the virtue of "the whole world for all people" as their lifelong moral pursuit.

In modern times, the Chinese communists and their leaders, such as Mao Zedong, Zhou Enlai, Liu Shaoqi, and Zhu De, were all remarkable representatives of the lofty spirit of "the whole world for all people." Since its founding, the Communist Party of China has taken the liberation of all mankind and realization of communism as its highest ideal and utmost goal. In his speech entitled "Serve

生不占民宅、死不占民田。他们都有一个共同点,那就是把"为公"作为始终如一的人生道德追求。

在现代,中国共产党人及毛泽东、周恩来、刘少奇、朱德等领袖群体,就是中华民族天下为公的正大精神的杰出代表。中国共产党从成立的第一天起,就开宗明义地把解放全人类,实现共产主义作为党的最高理想和最终目标。毛泽东主席在题为《为人民服务》的演讲中,提出"我们的共产党和共产党所领导的八路军、新四军,是革命的队伍。我们这个队伍完全是为着解放人民的,是彻底地为人民的利益工作的"。高度概括了中国共产党人所共同具有的天下为公的精神品质和崇高境界。经过共产党人不懈奋斗,开拓进取,更以无数共产党人的前赴后继、千千万万人的牺牲,换得新中国成立,中国人民终于站立起来,扬眉吐气追求新生活。

孙中山题"天下为公"
"The World Is Public" in Sun Yat-sen's Handwriting

党的十八大以来,中国不断为"天下为公"注入新时代内涵。行天下之大道,成为习近平新时代中国特色社会主义思想的一个鲜明特征。"为中国人民谋幸福"凸显"天下为公"的奉公为民精神,"为中华民族谋复兴"凸显"天下为公"的民族使命担当,"为世界谋大同"凸显"天下为公"的人文主义情怀。三"为"三"谋",是"天下为公"本质特征的政治价值、理论价值、人文价值和实践价值的集中彰显,是新时代中国共产党人行天下之大道的价值旗帜,是"四个自信"的生动

the People," Chairman Mao Zedong stated, "Our Communist Party and the Eighth Route Army and the New Fourth Army led by the Communist Party are a revolutionary force, working utterly for the liberation of the people and the interests of people." His statement summarized the lofty aim of "the whole world for all people" of the Communist Party of China. Through the unremitting struggle and sacrifice of communists, the People's Republic of China was founded, and the Chinese people finally arose to pursue a new life with pride and confidence.

Since the Eighteenth National Congress of the Communist Party of China, China has been injecting the new connotation into the concept of "the whole world for all people." Under the leadership of Xi Jinping, practicing good virtues to benefit the people has become a clear characteristic of socialism with Chinese characteristics in the new era. For example, "to seek happiness for the Chinese people" highlights the spirit of "pursuing public interests" in "the whole world for all people." "Seeking rejuvenation for the Chinese nation" punctuates China's national mission with this spirit, while "seeking great harmony for the world" stresses its humanistic sentiment. These new connotations embody the political, theoretical, humanistic, and practical values of the essential traits in "the whole world for all people," the flagship of performing good virtues by Chinese communists in the new era, and a vivid reflection of the "four confidences"—confidence in the path, confidence in the theories of the Party, confidence in the system of socialism with Chinese characteristics, and confidence in China's unique civilization. We should carry forward the spirit of "the whole world for all people" without wavering in the pursuit of the "concentric circle" of the above connotations. We must work together to promote the Chinese dream of national rejuvenation and the vision of a global community of shared future.

体现。弘扬"天下为公"行大道的精神,持之以恒画好三个"为"与"谋"的"同心圆",共同推进中华民族伟大复兴的中国梦与人类命运共同体的美好愿景更加紧密地彼此相依、携手并进、交相辉映。

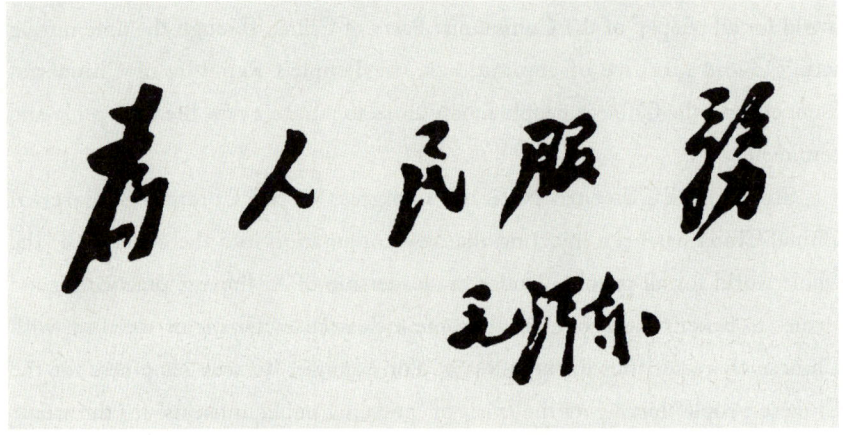

毛泽东题"为人民服务"
"Serve the People" in Mao Zedong's Handwriting

仰韶时期部落生活绘图
Tribal Life in the Yangshao Period

五、以人为本的人文精神

自黄帝始,中华文明便拉开了以人为中心的文明篇章,并代代传承发展。我国古籍中最早提出"以人为本"的是春秋时期齐国名相管仲,语见《管子·霸言》:"夫霸王之所始也,以人为本。本理则国固,本乱则国危。""以人为本"的内容包括"以人为尊""以民为贵""以仁为本"等,如《尚书·泰誓上》:"惟天地,万物父母;惟人,万物之灵。"清华简《厚父》说:"民心惟本,厥作惟叶。"《老子》二十五章:"故道大,天大,地大,人亦大。域中有四大,而人居其一焉。人法地,地法天,天法道,道法自然。"把人和道、天、地并列,为四大之一。《礼记·礼运》:"故人者,其天地之德,阴阳之交,鬼神之会,五行之秀气也。"从天地、阴阳、鬼神、五行等角度,肯定了人的崇高地位。《孔子家语·六本》:"天生万物,唯人为贵。"

人文精神的核心是"以人为本",即对人的尊崇,从治国理政方面讲,就是坚持以人民为中心,把满足人民群众的物质文化生活需要作为根本目标,使天下人安居乐业、丰衣足食、身心健康。黄帝文化精神标识与精髓中的"以人为本"思想主要体现在顺应规律、善政为民、肇造文明三个方面。

探索自然、顺应规律,改造生存环境、提升生活空间是黄帝人本思想的第一种体现。黄帝一生成功笃行的主要缘由就在于坚持了"顺天地之纪"的大原则,探索出了"人法地,地法天,天法道,道法自然"宇宙法则,进而创立天地大道,实现天地人和,成就丰功伟业。黄帝以人为本塑造龙的图腾,赋予龙中、和、容、实等人文特性,表现出合众为龙,日新为龙,万变成龙;有容为大,能和为大,执中为大;只有仁人顺民,才能成大成龙。黄帝从实际出发,遵循自然规律,道法自然又作用于自然,使得自然法则得到遵循,也使得人的主动性得以发挥。

V. People-Oriented Spirit

Since the Yellow Emperor era, Chinese civilization has developed a "people-oriented" civilization. According to ancient Chinese books, it was Guan Zhong, the famous minister of Qi State during the Spring and Autumn Period, who first put forward the concept of "people-oriented," which can be found in *Guanzi*, "The foundation of a great state is people-oriented. Following this idea, the state will be strong; otherwise, it will be in danger." This cannotation of people-orientedness includes "respect people," "people first," and "benevolence as the foundation." According to ancient Chinese books, it was Guan Zhong, the famous minister of Qi State during the Spring and Autumn Period, who first put forward the concept of "people-orientedness," which can be found in *Guanzi*, "The foundation of a great state is people-oriented. Following this idea, the state will be strong; otherwise, it will be in danger." For example, *Book of History* (an important Confucian classics) outlines that "heaven and earth are the parents of all living creatures while the human being is the brightest and noblest among all living creatures." On the Tsinghua Bamboo Slips *Houfu*, it is written that "people's will is the foundation of society, just as leaves are the essence of a plant." Chapter 25 of *Lao Tzu* states, "Therefore, the Tao is great, the heaven is great, the earth is great, and, hence, Man is also great. In the universe, there are four great objects, and Man is one among the four. Man follows the laws of the earth, the earth follows the laws of the heaven, the heaven follows the laws of the Tao, and the Tao follows the laws of nature." In *Book of Rites*, it is similarly written that "man is the result of the interaction between heaven and earth, between yin and yang, between ghosts and gods, and between the Five Elements." Hence, from the perspectives of heaven and earth, yin and yang, ghosts and gods, and the Five Elements, the status of man is affirmed. *The Confucian School's Analects* evinces that "of all living creatures, only man is the most creative."

The core of humanism is a "people-oriented" perspective—that is, "respect people." In terms of state governance, we must put people first and make it a fundamental goal to satisfy their material and cultural needs, helping people to live and work in peace, to have adequate living supplies, and to be physically and

善政为民是以人为本思想在黄帝文化精神标识与精髓中的第二种体现。我国传统的民本观念是相对于君本、官本而言的,其原意是指中国古代的明君、贤臣为维护和巩固统治而提出的一种统治观,其基本思想主要表现为重民、贵民、安民、恤民、爱民等。黄帝《巾几铭》说,黄帝深知"予居民上,摇摇恐夕不至朝,惕惕恐朝不及夕。兢兢慄慄,日慎一日",他始终把民情民利放在心上,努力为民谋利,建立和谐的君民关系。

黄帝民本思想的另一个重要体现是他尊重民意,善于采纳大众意见。《吕氏春秋·用众》载:"夫取于众,此三皇五帝之所以大立功名也。"史籍和传说记载了黄帝问道大隗、广成子,及黄帝与大臣讨论、请教执政、医学、星象等相关问题的事例。

《吕氏春秋》
Mister Lü's Spring and Autumn Annals

维护可持续发展是黄帝以人为本思想的另一重要体现。依据文献记载,昔时世处洪荒,民生草昧。黄帝以民为本,殚精竭虑,系统地创造出文明社会所需要的一系列物质和精神财富,并且使文明程度不断提

mentally healthy. The "people-oriented" idea reflected in the essence of Huangdi culture is manifested principally in three aspects: obedience to the law, good governance for the people, and the creation of civilization.

《管子》
Guanzi

Huangdi's humanist idea incorporates exploring nature, conforming to the law, and improving the living environment and space of the people. Huangdi's success lay primarily in his adherence to the principle of "conforming to the orders of nature," following his exploration of the universal law that "Man follows the laws of the earth, the earth follows the laws of the heaven, the heaven follows the laws of the Tao, and the Tao follows the laws of nature." He forged a way to realize harmony between heaven and earth, which resulted in great achievements. Huangdi valued men as the foundation for shaping the dragon totem, and endowed the dragon with humanistic characteristics, such as unity, harmony, tolerance, and realism, suggesting that unity, newness, and change were features of the dragon and that tolerance, harmony, and persistence were aspects of greatness. Only benevolence and adherence to the people-oriented ideal can help a nation expand and strengthen itself. Proceeding from the real situation he perceived around him, Huangdi conformed to the laws of nature, which, according to

高，保持持续发展的态势。《史记·五帝本纪》记载："顺天地之纪，幽明之占，死生之说，存亡之难。时播百谷草木，淳化鸟兽虫蛾，旁罗日月星辰水波土石金玉，劳勤心力耳目，节用水火材物，有土德之瑞，故号黄帝。"黄帝倡导的"节用水火材物"精神，要求人们对自然资源取之有时，用之有节，以永续利用，长享其利，这一可持续发展思想对中华民族的生息繁衍和社会文明进步发挥了积极作用。后世哲人在黄帝思想影响下对天人和谐思想不断充实丰富，传承发展。

在关注民情、致力民生方面，黄帝除了解决人民的衣食住行，还进行思想文化方面的培育，使人民安居乐业，幸福生活。黄帝的以人为本精神，是中国历朝历代执政者的一面镜子。从黄帝倡导"吾爱民而民不亡""为民立极""号令合于民心，则民听令"到颛顼的"养材以任地……治气以教民"；从帝喾"顺天之义，知民之急"到尧舜"孝慈仁爱，使民如子弟""敬授民时""以民为本"，经过五帝时代、夏商周时期的不断发展，到了春秋战国以降，成了儒家宣扬"仁政"思想和帝王执政理念的重要内容和守则。从孔子"富民、利民"到孟子"民为贵，社稷次之，君为轻"；从魏征"水能载舟亦能覆舟"到张载"为天地立心，为生民立命，为往圣继绝学，为万世开太平"，这些思想和主张，都与"以民为本"的人文主义密切相关。

张载画像
Portrait of Zhang Zai (a famous philosopher of the Northern Song Dynasty)

Taoism, acted on nature and thus motivated the people.

To govern for the people is the second manifestation of Huangdi's people-oriented thought. The traditional people-oriented concept in China was in comparison with the ruler-oriented and official-oriented concepts. People-oriented concept was proposed by virtuous rulers and officials in ancient China to maintain and consolidate political power. Its basic idea involved paying attention to, prioritizing, pacifying, understanding, and loving the people. Huangdi deeply appreciated the importance of the people; he strove for the best for them and built a harmonious relationship between the monarch and the people. In *Jinjiming*, Huangdi stated, "If I live above my people, I will have to be cautious all the time."

Respecting and adopting public opinion is another important manifestation of Huangdi's people-oriented thought. *Mister Lü's Spring and Autumn Annals* states, "Accepting public opinion is the key to the success of the Three Sovereigns and Five Emperors." Historical texts and legends recount instances when Huangdi consulted Dawei, Guangchengzi, and his ministers on issues related to governance, medicine, and astrology.

Maintaining sustainable development is another key feature of Huangdi's people-oriented thought. According to literature, in ancient times, people lived in darkness. Huangdi, who always put people first, worked hard to systematically create a series of material and spiritual cultural development necessary to civilization. Therefore, the level of civilization continued to improve, and society sustained development. *Records of the Grand Historian* states, "Huangdi conformed to heaven and earth to predict the change of yin and yang, to explain the orders of life and death, and to discuss the reasons for existence and nonexistence. Huangdi led his people to sow all kinds of grains and grasses according to the seasons and to tame birds and animals. He predicted natural phenomena and worked hard at collecting resources for civilian use. He had the auspicious signs of the attribute of earth, which is yellow in color, so he was called Huangdi, the Yellow Emperor." Huangdi's promotion of "resource-saving" led people to use resources appropriately in a sustainable way. This notion of sustainable development has played a positive role in the survival and development of the Chinese nation and social civilization. Later generations of philosophers continued to enrich the idea of a harmonious relationship between heaven and

黄帝的人文精神是中国历朝历代执政者的思想指南和座右铭，也是当代中国所大力弘扬的精神。从毛泽东所倡导的全心全意为人民服务，到江泽民的"三个代表"，从胡锦涛的"科学发展观"到习近平总书记所讲的"人民对美好生活的向往，就是我们的奋斗目标"，其执政理念始终是以人为本，是以人民的福祉为最高目标的人文精神体现。

习近平总书记在2016年省部级主要领导干部学习贯彻党的十八届五中全会精神专题研讨会上的讲话指出："要坚持人民主体地位，顺应人民群众对美好生活的向往，不断实现好、维护好、发展好最广大人民根本利益，做到发展为了人民、发展依靠人民、发展成果由人民共享。"习总书记的讲话，顺应人民呼声，直面群众诉求，致力于人民幸福生活。这种以民为本的执政理念，具有强大的人文精神感召力和凝聚力。它能集聚全民之力，使人民不懈奋斗，为实现中华民族的伟大复兴创造新辉煌。

人民文化生活缩影——打腰鼓
People's Cultural Life—Drum Dance

man developed in Huangdi culture.

Huangdi not only satisfied people's basic life necessities, but also educated them ideologically and culturally, so they could live and work peacefully and happily. His people-oriented spirit served as a mirror for the rulers of all following dynasties in China. Huangdi advocated "loving the people so that they would not die of hunger and fatigue," "setting up examples for the people," and making orders that "satisfy people's needs so that they can obey them." In a similar way, Zhuanxu "developed production according to different regional conditions… and cultivated people by creating the etiquette system." Emperor Ku "conformed to the orders of nature and understood people's needs." Likewise, Yao and Shun believed in "filial piety and benevolence so that people are like families," "conferred the calendar to the people so that they could farm according to seasons," and "put people first." After continuous development in the period of the Five Legendary Rulers, as well as the Xia, Shang, and Zhou dynasties, these concepts became important content and codes for Confucianism, promoting the idea of "benevolent governance" during the Spring and Autumn Period and the Warring States Period. From Confucius' "enriching the people and benefiting the people" to Mencius' "people first, society second, and the monarch last," and from Wei Zheng's "water can carry the boat, and it is able to overturn the boat" to Zhang Zai's "to ordain conscience for heaven and the earth, to secure life and fortune for the people, to inherit and carry forward the declining Confucian doctrine, and to establish peace for all future generations," Chinese ideas and propositions are closely tied to the people-oriented spirit.

Huangdi's humanistic spirit has been an ideological guide and motto of China's historical rulers and is still vigorously promoted today. From Mao Zedong's advocacy of serving the people wholeheartedly to Jiang Zemin's "Three Represents," as well as from Hu Jintao's "Scientific Outlook on Development" to General Secretary Xi Jinping's statement "To meet the desire of the people for a happy life is our mission," modern governance philosophies adhere to a people-oriented view, making people's welfare the ultimate goal and reflecting a humanistic spirit.

In 2016, General Secretary Xi Jinping observed, "We must maintain the people's principal position in the country, conform to the people's pursuit for a

在当代中国，党和政府以民为本的执政理念深入民心。从现阶段来看，政府正在解决基本民生问题，建立起人民生活的基本保障体系，包括文化、教育、就业、医疗、养老、住房等民生基本生活保障。

习近平总书记十分关注农村的改革与发展，他明确指出："中国要强，农业必须强；中国要美，农村必须美；中国要富，农民必须富。"习总书记用理论引导方向，用制度夯实基础，用文化凝聚人心，带领全国人民排除千难万险，终于走出了中国特色的农村城镇化之路。农民群众因地制宜创造乡村发展模式，提升乡村资源价值，拓展乡村发展空间，形成了促进农业强、农民富、农村美的长效发展机制。

据资料显示，1956年全国居民人均可支配收入只有98元，到2018年，这一数字已升至28228元。2019年，农村贫困人口数量从1978年的7.7亿减少至551万。作为首个完成联合国千年发展目标减贫目标的发展中国家，中国消灭贫困的实践被西方观察家誉为"人类历史上最伟大的故事之一"。中国在2020年已实现全面建成小康社会，这是人类历史上的一个伟大创举。

河南新郑阳光社区

Yangguang Community, Xinzheng, Henan Province

better life, and continue to serve, maintain and develop the fundamental interests of the overwhelming majority of the people, so that development is for the people, depends on the people, and the fruits of development are shared by the people." General Secretary Xi's speech responded to public opinion, addressed the demands of the people, and was devoted to satisfying their desire for a happy life. This people-oriented concept of governance is humanistic and cohesive. It can gather together the strength of the entire society, encourage the people to work tirelessly, and create new glory for China's rejuvenation.

In contemporary China, the people-oriented governance philosophy of both the Party and government is deeply rooted in the hearts of the people. At present, the government is addressing the basic issues of people's livelihoods and establishing a foundational security system for people's lives, including culture, education, employment, medical care, pensions, and housing.

General Secretary Xi Jinping is deeply concerned about the reform and development of rural areas. He clearly stated, "If China is to be strong, so is agriculture; if China is to be beautiful, so are the rural areas; if China is to be rich, so are farmers." In establishing ideal aims for the country, consolidating its foundation, and uniting the people, General Secretary Xi is leading the people to overcome various difficulties and dangers and embark on a path of rural urbanization in a characteristically Chinese way. Farmers are creating a rural development model in accordance with local conditions, enhancing the value of rural resources, and expanding the space for rural development, resulting in a long-term development mechanism with strong agricultural systems, rich farmers, and beautiful rural areas.

According to statistics, the per capita disposable income of Chinese residents was only 98 yuan in 1956. By 2018, it had risen to 28,228 yuan. The number of people living in poverty in rural areas decreased from 770 million in 1978 to 5.51 million in 2019. As the first developing country to complete the poverty alleviation goal of the United Nations MDGs, China's practice in poverty alleviation has been hailed by Western observers as "one of the greatest stories in human history." China has comprehensively achieved the goal of a moderately prosperous society in 2020, which is also a significant achievement in human history.

六、中和大同的和谐精神

"中和",即中正和谐。"致中和",则天地万物均能各得其所,达于和谐境界。"中"即适度,"和"即和谐融合,两者是"体"与"用"的关系,即内在本质与外在表现的关系。世间万物的发展变化如果保持适度适中,就可以达到事物总体的和。"大同"社会是古代儒家所宣扬的理想社会,是说人人都能受到全社会的关爱。"不独亲其亲,不独子其子",每个人都能推己及人,把奉养父母、抚育儿女的心意扩大到其他人,使全社会亲如一家。

"和谐"是指和睦协调,和好相处。和谐社会是指一种美好的社会状态和一种美好的社会理想,即形成全体人民各尽其能、各得其所而又和谐相处的社会。中和大同的和谐精神,其渊源可追溯到黄帝时代。"故黄帝作君臣上下之义,父子兄弟之礼,夫妇妃匹之合。"让人民各明其分,各安其位,各行其是,建立起和顺的家庭和社会关系。黄帝不仅行仁义,重德治,和人心,而且也影响周边古国。随着中和政策的实施,最终统一天下,使各族的文化前所未有地,有效地,潜移默化地进行着交流与融合。黄帝所言的"观天之道,执天之行""立天之道,以定人也"(《黄帝阴符经》),彰显出天人合一、人与自然的和谐观。

黄帝的中和思想在于名理。"名理者,循名究理之所之",就是说,既要在行事中循名究理,还要在理论和方法上把握它的内在实质。理,就是事物的条理、准则,即事物所蕴含的特性。名理可以确定是非的分际,然后以法度为依据去裁决。凡事以近情理为目的,凭常识而论实际,反对偏倚,反对极端,宽容忍耐,趋于妥协恰当。所以,黄帝认为"应化之道,平衡而止""轻重不符,是为失道""赢极不静,是为失道""内外皆顺,命曰天当""动静不时,妄动必患""取予得体,便是得当"。得当便是正确、正当、妥当、中和、和合。

VI. Spirit of Great Unity

"Great unity" (Zhong He) signifies unity and harmony. "To unite" signifies that every creature in the world fulfills its wish and reaches a state of harmony. The Chinese character "Zhong" means moderate, and "He" means harmony. The two concepts embody the relationship between "body" and "use," which indicates the relationship between essence and appearance. If the development of all things in the world is moderate, a state of harmony can be achieved. A "greatly united" society is the ideal form of society promoted by ancient Confucians in which everyone is taken care of and loved by society as a whole: "Thus people do not treat only their parents like parents, nor do people treat only their sons like sons." Everyone can place themselves in others' shoes and extend their love from parents and children to other people, making the whole society as close as a family.

"Harmony" refers to be compatible. A harmonious society refers to a society in which everyone does his best, fulfills his goals, obtains what he seeks, and lives in accord with. The spirit of "great unity" can be traced back to the Yellow Emperor era, "So Huangdi formulated the ranks of the king and the ministers, the rites of father and son, and the marriage of husband and wife." This social organization allowed people to understand their own responsibilities, work on their own positions, and perform their own duties, forming the premise for harmonious family and social relationships. Huangdi not only practiced benevolence and righteousness, ruling with virtue and uniting his own tribe, but also influenced surrounding tribes. By implementing a neutralization policy, Huangdi finally unified the country, merged cultures, and encouraged cultural exchange from every tribe in an unprecedented, effective, and subtle way. His interests in "observing the way of nature and practicing in accordance to the way of the nature" and "determining the human nature through the way of nature" (cf. *Huangdi Yinfujing*) demonstrate the harmony between man and nature.

Huangdi's ideal of unity and harmony lies in understanding. "Understanding is to find out the reasons behind matters." In other words, we must not only understand the reason for a matter, but also ascertain its essence in theory and method. Reason is the way things are, that is, the characteristics that things imply.

《黄帝阴符经》
Huangdi Yinfujing

　　黄帝文化是历史的、多样的、多层次的立体文化。它为各民族新文化的发展提供了多样的选择，改变着自身的文化内容和形式。就黄帝时代而言，由于民族的融合统一，社会秩序井然，人民安居乐业，社会祥和，逐渐形成了由以前的多源、多向和思想的多样化，向多样一体、视界融合、交互作用、融合统一的方面转化。这种转化，与各民族人民的知识结构、认知方式、心理状态、生活体验有关。这种视界和心理的统一，使得当时的文化逐步叠加累积发展起来，成为各族人民共同享有的文化。这种在时代变迁中融合形成的和谐文化以及文化环境，对于人际交往、辨识意识的形成，都起着决定性的作用。

　　以黄帝和谐文化而论，我们在经典中发现，人与自然之天、之地、之水、草木鸟兽都是相依相融的。天、地、人、物不是各自独立、相互对峙的系统，而是彼此之间有着不可分割的关系，人与万物是一个密不可分的整体。人不与自然对立，讲求的是与自然和谐共处。据《黄帝四经·十大经·前道》可知，君主要想称王天下，就必

Understanding reason helps one to tell right from wrong and to judge on the basis of law. All things should be judged reasonably and discussed according to common sense. Biases and extremes should be avoided, and tolerance and compromise should be encouraged. Accordingly, Huangdi believed that "we should follow changes and maintain balance," "not knowing the severity of a matter is unjust," "to win without peace is unjust," "internal governance and diplomacy should comply with the order of heaven," "movements should be appropriate, otherwise they will cause danger," and "to receive and give appropriately is right." To Huangdi, therefore, the right way of governance was correct, just, proper, neutral, and harmonious.

Huangdi culture is a historical, diverse, and multi-level culture with numerous dimensions. It provides various options for the development of new cultures of different nationalities, which thereafter change their own cultures and forms. In the Yellow Emperor era, the integration and unity of nations led to an orderly society in which people could live happily. Huangdi culture has gradually transformed from a diversified ideology to an integration of diversity, interaction, and unity. This transformation is related to the knowledge structure, cognitive style, mental state, and life experience of people originating from various nationalities. This unification of vision and psychology allowed the culture to accumulate and develop gradually, finally evolving into a culture shared by all nationalities. The harmonious culture and cultural environment formed by cultural fusion over time play a decisive role in the formation of interpersonal communication and recognition.

Regarding the harmonious culture of Huangdi, classic texts show that men are interdependent with sky, land, water, vegetation, birds, and beasts. Heaven, earth, men, and objects are neither independent of each other nor in conflict with each other. Men are not the opposite of nature but aim to live in harmony with nature. According to *Four Texts of Huangdi*, if the monarch wants to rule the world, he must be concerned with three factors: time, location, and person. "To govern the country, one must obey the established rules, i.e., to know the time, the location and the person," and then the world is united. This statement illustrates a cultural consciousness of the monarch's participation in the harmony of heaven, earth, and men. The harmony between men and heaven promotes the human

须权衡参合天时、地利、人事三方面的因素。又"治国固有前道,上知天时,下知地利,中知人事",然后才能广有天下。这里表达的是王者参合天、地、人事的文化自觉,是人与天的和谐,把人的精神提升到超脱寻常的人与我、物与我之分别的"天人合一"之境。道、天、地、人是宇宙间的四种伟大存在,人以地为法则,地以天为法则,天以道为法则,道以它自己的样子为法则。就是说,人要因地制宜,用地要根据天时的变化,变化有自然界的规律性。"道"是天地自然的总规律与总过程,所以,王者既要遵循天道的规律,又要向人道倾斜,然后合于民心,合于民心谓之和顺。

黄帝文化"天人合一"的实质即是和谐。而这种和谐,一是人与自然的和谐,二是人与人的和谐,三是人与精神世界、内在自我、身心的和谐。这三大和谐揭示出了黄帝和谐文化的人文向度和哲学高度。

中华文化,是不同地域文化的综合,诸如中原的仰韶文化、龙山文化,东南的良渚文化等,陆续融入其中,发展壮大起来,形成多样一体的文化形态。在这个过程中,以黄帝为代表的华夏文化逐渐崛起,并占据了主导地位。经过夏、商、周三代,华夏文化所在的黄河中下游成为中华文化的中心。黄帝文化是中华文化的根和源,更是中华文化的象征。黄帝文化经过融合、发展,已经得到中华民族的广泛认同,它成了中华各族人民共同创造的文明,这正是多样一体的中华民族文化。

和谐精神是中华优秀传统文化的重要核心内容。它为中华民族生生不息、自立自强、开拓进取、发展壮大提供了强大精神动力。在中国历史上,黄帝的和谐文化不断继承发展、发扬光大。殷周时期,"和合"二字就已出现,春秋时期,"和合"二字联用,构成了和合范畴。《国语·郑语》说:"商契能和合五教,以保于百姓者也。"道家创始人老子,提出了"万物负阴而抱阳,冲气以为和"的主张,认为万物都包含着阴阳,阴阳相互作用而构成和。

spirit to the "harmony of nature and men" that is beyond the ordinary harmony between man and self, as well as between objects and self. Tao, heaven, earth, and men are the four great existences in the universe. Man follows the laws of the earth, the earth follows the laws of heaven, heaven follows the laws of the Tao, and the Tao follows the laws of nature. In other words, people must adapt to local conditions, use land based on changes in the weather, and follow certain orders of nature to make changes. "Tao" is the general law and process of heaven and earth. Therefore, the monarch must not only follow the order of heaven but also the order of men and listen to public opinion; this process culminates in harmony.

Harmony is the essence of the "integration of man and nature" in Huangdi culture. It contains the following three states: harmony between man and nature; harmony among men; harmony between men, the spiritual world, the inner self, body, and mind. These three states of harmony reveal the humanistic dimension and philosophy of Huangdi's harmonious culture.

Chinese culture is an integration of the following different regional cultures: Yangshao Culture and Longshan Culture from the Central Plains and Liangzhu Culture in the southeast, which evolved over time and finally converged into one diverse and integrated culture. Through this process, the Chinese culture represented by Huangdi was formed and occupied a dominant position in the overall culture of the Chinese nation. After the Xia, Shang, and Zhou dynasties, the middle and lower reaches of the Yellow River, where Chinese culture was developed, became the center of Chinese culture. Huangdi culture is, therefore, the root and source, as well as a symbol, of Chinese culture. Through integration and development, Huangdi culture has been widely recognized by the Chinese nation, representing a civilization created by people of all nationalities in China and reflecting the simultaneous diversity and cohesion of Chinese national culture.

The spirit of harmony provides a powerful spiritual motivation for the Chinese nation to thrive, improve, forge ahead, and grow. Throughout the Chinese history, Huangdi's harmonious culture has continued to develop and thrive. "Harmony" and "unity" appeared as early as the Yin and Zhou dynasties, and the terms were used together to form a unified idea in the Spring and Autumn Period. The founder of Taoism, Lao Tzu, proposed that "everything has a bright side and a dark side, coexistent in harmony," indicating that yin and yang are contained in

老子像
Portrait of Lao Tzu

儒家学派创始人孔子说:"君子和而不同,小人同而不和。""和"是宇宙万物的本质和天地万物生存的基础。《管子》说:"畜之以道,则民和;养之以德,则民合。和合故能习。"认为遵从道德,人民就和合,达至团聚、和谐。墨子说:"离散不能相和合。"并指出要安定天下,不能有离散之心。秦汉以降,中国文化的发展更呈现出一种和谐发展的趋势。不仅各家各派讲和谐,而且儒、道在保持各自文化特点的同时,相互吸取、融合,由此促进了中国和谐文化的可持续发展。

在当今科技高度发展的信息时代,构建和谐社会已成为中华民族走向复兴、矗立于世界民族之林的重要方略。习近平总书记十分重视中华和谐文化思想建设。他在联合国教科文组织进行访问时,作了重要演讲。他说:"文明是多彩的,人类文明因多样才有交流互鉴的价值""文明是平等的,人类文明因平等才有交流互鉴的前提""文明是

everything and that their interaction constitutes harmony.

Confucius, the founder of Confucianism, said, "A gentleman seeks harmony from difference, and a villain seeks difference from harmony." "Harmony" is the essence of all objects in the universe and the foundation for the existence of all things. Similarly, *Guanzi* observed, "People with morality will live in harmony; people who are raised by virtues will live in unity. Therefore, harmony and unity can be achieved through practice." According to him, by following morals, people are united and harmonious. Taking another angle, Mozi stated "people with the mind of separation cannot be reconciled," noting that to stabilize the world, one cannot seek to separate. Since the Qin and Han dynasties, Chinese culture has shown a trend of harmonious development. Not only do various schools of thought advocate harmony, but Confucianism and Taoism absorb and merge with each other while maintaining their respective cultural characteristics, thus promoting the sustainable development of a harmonious Chinese culture.

In the current advanced information age, building a harmonious society has become a crucial strategy for the Chinese nation to rejuvenate and stand among the nations of the world. General Secretary Xi Jinping attaches significant importance to the values and construction of a concordant Chinese culture. In this speech during a visit to United Nations Educational, Scientific, and Cultural Organization (UNESCO), he stated, "Civilizations are colorful, and such diversity has made exchanges and mutual learning among civilizations relevant and valuable; civilizations are equal, and such equality has made exchanges and mutual learning among civilizations possible; civilizations are inclusive, and such inclusiveness has given exchanges and mutual learning among civilizations the needed drive to move forward. Only by interacting with and learning from others can a civilization enjoy full vitality... If all civilizations can uphold inclusiveness, the so-called 'clash of civilizations' will be out of the question, and the harmony of civilizations will become reality." General Secretary Xi Jinping's speech called for "a civilizational perspective of equality, mutual learning, dialogue, and inclusiveness among civilizations," pointing to a path for the harmonious coexistence of human civilizations. It highlighted the importance of mutual trust, mutual benefit, equality, consultation, respect for diverse civilizations, and common development to a harmonious culture.

包容的，人类文明因包容才有交流互鉴的动力……只有交流互鉴，一种文明才能充满生命力。只要秉持包容精神，就不存在什么'文明冲突'，就可以实现文明和谐"。习近平总书记的演讲，呼吁要"弘扬平等、互鉴、对话、包容的文明观"，指出了一条人类文明和谐共生之路，同时也阐释了和谐文化所主张的互信、互利、平等、协商，尊重多样文明、谋求共同发展的重要内涵。

在当今中国，大力弘扬黄帝中和大同的和谐精神，对构建世界命运共同体，推动祖国和平统一，实现中华民族伟大复兴，定能起到巨大的促进作用。

In today's China, the spirit of great unity is vigorously promoted. This spirit will play an central role in building a global community of shared future, promoting the peaceful reunification of the country, and realizing the great rejuvenation of the Chinese nation.

附录：中国历史年代简表

Appendix: A Brief Chronology of Chinese History

中国历史年代简表
A Brief Chronology of Chinese History

五帝时代 Period of the Five Legendary Rulers c. 2600 BC-c. 2070 BC	黄帝 Huangdi (Yellow Emperor)	
	颛顼 Zhuanxu	
	帝喾 Diku (Emperor Ku)	
	尧 Yao	
	舜 Shun	
夏 Xia Dynasty	c. 2070 BC-c. 1600 BC	
商 Shang Dynasty	c. 1600 BC-c. 1046 BC	
西周 Western Zhou Dynasty	c. 1046 BC-c. 771 BC	
东周 Eastern Zhou Dynasty 770 BC-256 BC	春秋 Spring and Autumn Period	770 BC-476 BC
	战国 Warring States Period	475 BC-221 BC
秦 Qin Dynasty	221 BC-206 BC	
汉 Han Dynasty 206 BC-220 AD	西汉 Western Han	206 BC-25 AD
	东汉 Eastern Han	25 AD-220 AD
三国 Three Kingdoms 220 AD-280 AD	魏 Wei	220 AD-265 AD
	蜀汉 Shu Han	221 AD-263 AD
	吴 Wu	222 AD-280 AD
晋 Jin Dynasty 265 AD-420 AD	西晋 Western Jin	265 AD-317 AD
	东晋 Eastern Jin	317 AD-420 AD

续表 Continued Table

南北朝 Southern and Northern Dynasties 420 AD-589 AD	南朝 Southern Dynasties	宋 Song	420 AD-479 AD
		齐 Qi	479 AD-502 AD
		梁 Liang	502 AD-557 AD
		陈 Chen	557 AD-589 AD
	北朝 Northern Dynasties	北魏 Northern Wei	386 AD-534 AD
		东魏 Eastern Wei	534 AD-550 AD
		北齐 Northern Qi	550 AD-577 AD
		西魏 Western Wei	535 AD-556 AD
		北周 Northern Zhou	557 AD-581 AD
隋 Sui Dynasty		581 AD-618 AD	
唐 Tang Dynasty		618 AD-907 AD	
五代十国 Five Dynasties and Ten States	五代 Five Dynasties 907 AD-960 AD	后梁 Later Liang	907 AD-923 AD
		后唐 Later Tang	923 AD-936 AD
		后晋 Later Jin	936 AD-947 AD
		后汉 Later Han	947 AD-950 AD
		后周 Later Zhou	951 AD-960 AD
	十国 Ten States 902 AD-979 AD	北汉 Northern Han	951 AD-979 AD
		吴 Wu	902 AD-937 AD
		吴越 Wuyue	907 AD-978 AD
		闽 Min	909 AD-945 AD
		南汉 Southern Han	917 AD-971 AD
		荆南（又称"南平"）Jingnan (Nanping)	924 AD-963 AD
		楚 Chu	927 AD-951 AD
		南唐 Southern Tang	937 AD-975 AD
		前蜀 Former Shu	907 AD-925 AD
		后蜀 Later Shu	934 AD-965 AD

续表 Continued Table

宋 Song Dynasty 960 AD-1279 AD	北宋 Northern Song	960 AD-1127 AD
	南宋 Southern Song	1127 AD-1279 AD
辽 Liao (契丹 Qidan/Khitan)	907 AD-1125 AD	
西夏 Xixia (Tangut)	1038 AD-1227 AD	
金 Jin	1115 AD-1234 AD	
元 Yuan Dynasty	1206 AD-1368 AD	
明 Ming Dynasty	1368 AD-1644 AD	
清 Qing Dynasty	1616 AD-1911 AD	
中华民国 Republic of China	1912 AD-1949 AD	
中华人民共和国 People's Republic of China	1949 AD-